HILL KORWAS OF CHHATISGARH

Hill Korwas of Chhatisgarh

B.R. RIZVI

GYAN PUBLISHING HOUSE
New Delhi - 110002

Hill Korwas of Chhatisgarh

ISBN : 9788121202602

B.R. Rizvi

Published in 2016 in India by
Gyan Publishing House
5, Ansari Road, Daryaganj,
New Delhi - 110002
Phones : 23261060, 23282060 Fax : 23285914
e-mail : books@gyanbooks.com
website : gyanbooks.com

Laser Typesetting at : **Vinayak Printers, Delhi**
Printed at : **Salasar Imaging System, Delhi**

Dedicated

To

My wife

RIZWANA

Acknowledgement

Had it not been for the enthusiasm, encouragement and guidance extended by Dr. A.K. Danda whose pains-taking interest was a perennial source of inspiration for this author, this work would have not seen the light of the day. Words can hardly express the author's gratitude to him.

The Director, Anthropological Survey of India, kindly allowed the author to utilise the data collected from Chattisgarh Area Project in his dissertation. He was also kind enough to supply photo-plates and photo-copies used in this book. The author is thankful to him.

A number of friends and colleagues helped me while the work was in progress. I am specially thankful to Dr. Francis Ekka, Dr. Raj Shekhar and Mr. N.H. Itagi of Central Institute of Indian Languages, Mysore and to his colleagues Dr. P.K. Misra, Dr. M.K. Raha, Mr. M.N. Kaul, Mr. A.L. Deshpandey, Mr. S.S. Sastry, Mr. Arun Kumar Singh and Mr. B.K. Rajkumar.

Mr. K.N. Chandra Kant took pains to type the manuscript for which I am grateful to him.

Needless to mention, I am grateful to the Hill Korwas of Chhattisgarh who accepted me as one of their own and with whom I spent some of the best moments of my life.

B.R. RIZVI

Preface

This book presents an account of a primitive tribe practising food-gathering, hunting and shifting cultivation. It is among the first to describe such a tribe in an analytical frame of reference covering the first 25 years of India's independence. This study has an added significance, especially when the Government of India is giving more and more attention to the development of the tribal population of the country. It is a methodical analysis of not only the economic structure but also the social and ritual life of the tribe. The origin of the tribe has been described with its various clan names. Details of housing pattern, implements used for earning their livelihood, including fishing traps, bird traps, and weapons, etc.. The description of the dress pattern of the tribe suggests that they have not been influenced by the more developed tribal population or the Hindu population.

The description of the life-cycle has been described by the help of case studies. Economically, the Hill Korwa mainly depend on the forest resources although they have been provided with agricultural lands in the mid fifties of this century. One of the reasons for the economic backwardness of these people is the inferior quality of land and non-availability of irrigation facilities and lack of approach from extension officials to educate them about how to improve their agricultural productivity by using modern inputs. Considering the average size of the holdings of the family, it can be considered that if they are provided with proper guidance and financial assistance they can improve their economic and social life significantly. Traders, moneylenders, distillary owners, and big landlords exploit the Hill Korwa because of their illiteracy and ignorance and non-existance of financial institutions from where they could mobilise necessary funds on easy terms.

The study brings out some of the serious constraints which stand in the way of socio-economic development of the tribe such as lack of educational opportunities, lack of employment opportunities, and lack of transport and communication facilities, etc.

This work would have not seen the light of the day but for the encouragement shown by the Director General, Anthropological Survey of India for an early publication. I express my gratitude to Dr. A.K. Danga, Director, Anthropological Survey of India, who provided me an opportunity to work among the Hill Korwa and has always been a perennial source of inspiration to me. Many other friends and colleagues helped me immensely : the foremost among them was Prof. P.K. Mishra, North-Eastern Hill University, Shillong, Dr. A.K. Singh, Human Ecologist, Mr. M.N. Kaul, Statistician, Mr. Chandra Kant, who painstakingly typed the manuscript and Mr. Deshpande of Anthropological Survey of India. Dr. Francis Ekka, Central Institute of Indian Languages, Mysore was kind enough to put the services of Mr. Ingti, Cartographer, C.I.I.L., Mysore for preparing maps. Dr. Rajshekhar offered his valuable comments. In the last but not the least I express my gratitude to my wife Rizwana who spent many a sleepless nights with me when this book was under preparation and enlightened me with her valuable comments. I am thankful to them all. It will be an act of thanklessness and ingratitude if I do not remember and thank my Hill Korwa friends in whose company I spent eight memorable months as one of their own kin. I am also thankful to Mr. B.P. Garg of Gian Publishing House, New Delhi, for arranging publication of this book.

B.R. Rizvi

Contents

	Acknowledgement	vii
	Preface	ix
	List of Illustrations	xv
	List of Tables	xvii
1.	Introduction	1
2.	The People	29
3.	Economic Resources	103
4.	Economic Activities	125
5.	Economic Relationship	147
6.	Changing Economy	167
7.	The Hill Korwa at Cross Roads : Suggestions and Prospects	179
	Appendix	187-198
	Bibliography	199-204
	Glossary of Local Terms	205-212
	Index	213-216
	Illustrations	217-226

List of Illustrations

1. An elderly Chief (*mukhya*).
2. A Nascent household.
3. A nuclear household.
4. Mixing blood of the sacrificial chicken with millets for preservation till the next harvest (*ponti*).
5. Diviner (*Dewar*) performing Navagrahi worship.
6. ORNAMENTS : Guria, Hansuli, Phundna, Tarkula, Tarki, Angoothi, Phundna.
7. TRAPS : I Fishing Trap : *Mandra*
II Bird Trap : *Lassa Phanda*
III Fishing Trap : *Hatta*
8. Implements of hunting and self-defence : Tangi, Balua, Tangi, Tabal, Dhanu, Tir, Beetha, Bissar, Tangi.
9. Preserving a young sapling by planting it inside a hollowed treetrunk (*doli*).
10. A young bride.
11. A marriage party in progress.

List of Tables

	CHAPTER II	Pages
Table 2.1	Prohibited and permissible items of Korwa food	38
Table 2.2	Etymology of Korwa Names	41
Table 2.3	Korwa Names after months	42
Table 2.4	Methods of acquiring mates	60
Table 2.5	Incidences of clan endogamy	64
Table 2.6	Distribution of population according to clans	73
Table 2.7	Distribution of Korwa Households	77
Table 2.8	Household size according to members	84
Table 2.9	Changes in Korwa kinship terminology	88
Table 2.10	Korwa kinship terminology	89
	CHAPTER III	
Table 3.1	Land types in Chhattisgarh	105
Table 3.2	Number of landowning and landless Korwa households	107
Table 3.3	Distribution of households by size of land-holdings	108
Table 3.4	Size of landholdings per household, per Capita	110
Table 3.5	Percentage distribution of labour	111
Table 3.6	Division of labour	113
Table 3.7	Percentage of Agriculture Labourers	115
Table 3.8	Distribution of cattle owning and non-cattle owning households	118

Table 3.9 Animal wealth 119
Table 3.10 Economic resources 121

CHAPTER IV

Table 4.1 Food gathering schedule 133
Table 4.2 Worship of Pir-Deo 141
Table 4.3 Worship of deities responsible for higher yields 142

CHAPTER V

Table 5.1 Barter rate in Korwa villages 152
Table 5.2 Indebtedness Among the Hill Korwa 154

CHAPTER ONE

Introduction

nterest among anthropologists in studying the economic organizational network of smaller societies is a relatively recent phenomenon. Despite the existence of a few of classic studies in the field, 'primitive' economy has remained one of the most neglected areas of anthropological enquiry, particularly in India. Today, however, an increasing number of anthropologists are showing awareness of the importance of economic studies for better comprehension of the mechanism of the social system. But since few anthropologists have had any serious training in economic theory, often they have no clear idea about the kind of data they are required to collect from the field and how to compile and present the material thus collected. Marshall[1] describes the economics of 'savage' societies in the following terms:

'Scanty and untrustworthy as our information about the habits of savage tribes, we know enough of them to be sure that they show a strange uniformity of general characters, amid great variety of details...we find savages living under the dominion of custom and impulse; scarcely ever striking out new lines for themselves, never forecasting the distant future, and seldom making provision even for the near future...ready at times for the most arduous exertions......but incapable of keeping themselves along to steady work; those which are inevitable are done by the compulsory labour of women'.

No doubt, there were less anthropological studies of 'savage' societies when the above comments were made. But such studies have not largely been taken seriously by economists. The indifference expressed by Marshall may, thus, be explained due to the difference in methods, approaches, and commitments of students of different disciplines.

The methodological approach of economics differs greatly from that of anthropology. Much of the modern economics tends to be concerned mainly with the macrocosmic studies carried out with carefully prepared sampling techniques based on available statistics. By contrast, an anthropologist often focuses attention to a small unit which he examines in totality. This leads one to the most fundamental question regarding applicability of the tools of analysis, that have been developed in the context of industrial and market economics for studying preliterate societies organised on very different principles.

Opinions differ on this basic question. Danda[2] gives a vivid description of the controversy that economic anthropology has passed through during the recent decade. The major impetus for examining the effectiveness of tools of economic enquiry to simpler and smaller societies came from the publication of '*Trade and Market in Early Empires*'[3]. In recent decades, thus, economic anthropology experienced the growth of substantivist-formalist approaches which have resulted in major theoretical debate. Substantive economy, according to Polanyi[4] is derived from fact. It implies neither choice nor insufficiency of means and is based on the laws of nature. Formal economy on the other hand, is derived from logic. It has a set of rules referring to choice between alternative uses of insufficient means. Thus formal economy is based on the abstract models. Dalton[5] in his analysis of primitive economy, observes constraints on individual transactions. So, he employes the concept 'socio-economy' instead of 'economy' to interpret data of primitive economic system. In support of his views he refers to the dichotomy of Lewis[6] 'non-market' and 'market' economy and Firth's[7] 'economic aspect of social relations and economic transactions'. Barnett[8], Epstein[9], and Samuelson[10] though do not evolve any dichotomy of concepts, support the stand taken by the substantivists.

Formalists, among economic anthropologists have firm faith in the general applicability of economic principles and thus they rule out the possibility of the existence of multiple economic systems. Cook[11] claims that "the 'formalists' from Firth to Salisbury and Belshaw have successfully used the categories, concepts and principles of bourgeois economics in their studies of non-bourgeois forms of society with Marx's programme, i.e., without confusing social morphology with cultural content and context". Le Clair[12], Nash[13] & Panoff[14] may also be termed as formalists.

There is a category of social scientists who strongly feel that the differences between the viewpoints of substantivists and formalists are not as sharp as to justify a clear distinction between market and non-market economics.

Benett[15], a formalist observes, "...though there is a recognised difference between the conduct of the national and local economy, there is no justification for the theoretical position that proposes a sharp dichotomy between 'market' and 'non-market' economies." "What is needed", according to Kaplan[16] "is an approach which strives to achieve the generality of the 'formalists' while at the same time keeping a firm foothold in the empirical world—an approach that in the spirit of acumenism might be called 'substantive formalism' and 'formal substantivism'."

Bailey[17] while discussing 'the non-economic activities correlated it with capital saving and credit' and in 'A village of Highland Orissa' observes: "What social anthropology has to say to economics is that 'economic man' is also a social and political man, someone's husband, brother, and father, sometimes given to religious irrationality and so forth. But while this proposition has been agreed across the table, this agreement does not emerge in action".

Danda[18] without drawing himself into the above mentioned controversy finds "the simultaneous existence of the elements of micro-economy and macro-economy in a non-western society". It is a fact, he continues, "that the modern market system and the impact of western monetary system have penetrated even in the remote tribal areas. Still, so far they have not been able to completely replace the traditional methods of transaction and economic relationships that are socially obligatory and guided by mores and values of the respective societies."

A rapid glance over studies based on tribal economy in India reveals that all such studies are not specialised in nature. The majority of them are generalised and descriptive having information on tribal economy and/or their transformations. Some of the specialised studies do not entirely or exclusively deal with the tribal economy. With the passage of time there has been a steady growth of literature on this subject and in the twenties of the present century specific studies have started appearing. This trend continued till India became free from the alien rule. With the dawn of independence and the period that immediately followed a sudden spurt of literature both generalised and specialised in nature has been recorded and the rate of growth of specialised studies has been higher than that of the generalised studies. This newly developed interest may be attributed to anthropologists', politicians' and administrators' concern to get a clear picture of the economy for the most down-trodden hitherto ignored tribals of India and their efforts to ameliorate them their lot.

The earliest specialised study is that of Roy[19] on the Oraons of Chotanagpur, their history, economic life and social organization. The author has discussed the village organization and economic life of the people specifying various occupations followed by them. A detailed analysis of the mode of transactions and marketing has also been incorporated in the study. The earliest of its kind to deal with tribal economy, this study is unique and fairly detailed in nature but it is not a specialised study of the aspects of economy.

The year 1930 saw the appearance of a single specialised item by Majumdar[20] which entirely devoted itself to the economic background of social institutions in primitive societies and thus falls under the category of specialised studies on tribal economy. Dutta Majumdar[21] had his interest primarily in exploring the mode of transaction of goods by the Bhotias highlighting the importance of interdependence in tribal economy.

A major shift has however come in the forties. During earlier periods, the major concern was to examine self-sufficiency vis-a-vis interdependence in tribal economy. The contributors of the forties by and large engaged themselves in the investigation of the transferral process of the economic scene of the tribals and its consequences upon the people concerned. Chattopadhyaya[22], Dube[23], Furer-Haimendorf[24] and Husain[25] may be referred to as examples.

Further diversification of interest has been recorded in the period that followed 1950. Studies on tribal economy continued to be one of the major concerns with a special emphasis on change in tribal economy. Evaluative studies dealing with developmental measures were introduced as a part of planned change. Apte[26], Nag[27] and Mukherjee[28] belong to this category. Another major attempt in the field of tribal economy has been made by Singh.[28A] whose main focus is on change and transformation of the modes of production in tribal India induding the relations of production.

It may not be out of place to have a glance on the state of tribal economy in India in general and Chattisgarh in particular.

According to the report of the Commissioner, Scheduled Castes and Scheduled Tribes,[29] more than three fourths of the Scheduled Tribes are engaged in agriculture in one form or the other. Nearly 68 per cent of the tribal population in India is engaged in cultivation and 19.7 per cent are serving as agricultural labourers. In Nagaland and NEFA shifting cultivation is largely in vogue. In portions of Orissa and Madhya Pradesh slash and burn cultivation survives in association with more advanced forms of cultivation with the help of plough. The majority of the tribes who depend upon the former have either switched over to the plough cultivation or have been reduced to the position of farm labourers in the land which is owned by others in the neighbouring villages. Peasants from the plains have also gradually penetrated along the valleys into the mountainous areas and have engaged the former shifting cultivators either to produce special crops on their hills or serve them as labourers in the valley below.

The Andaman Islanders form a part of Indian population. Their total population is perhaps no more than one thuosand in Great and Little Andamans and Sentinel Islands etc. They live completely by hunting, fishing, and food gathering.

In the Western Himalayas comprising the provinces of U.P. Hills, Himachal Pradesh and Jammu and Kashmir, the tribal economy is based mainly on terrace cultivation and trade. Their pastoral way of life merges with agriculture. In Jammu and Kashmir, although there is no Scheduled Tribe, the main occupation of the people is agriculture.

Thus we see that the tribal economy in India is based on hunting, fishing, food gathering, shifting cultivation, and plough cultivation. Pastoralism is mixed with some of the above mentioned economic pursuits.

Coming to the Chattisgarh scenario, the observations made by Danda[30] on the tribal economy of Chattisgarh are very revealng: "Though Chattisgarh as a whole forms an important paddy growing area of Madhya Pradesh, in the agricultural map of India, this portion of the country is generally shown as the area under shifting cultivation. This is largely due to the agricultural practices of tribes like Baiga, Kodaku, Korwa and Nagesia, who even in the recent past used to do shifting cultivation. Today a large section of these people follow this method of cultivation when such opportunities are available. However, taking tribes together subsistence agriculture is the economic way of life of the people of Chattisgarh."

Objectives

The main purpose behind selecting this tribe has been enumerated below :

(a) The Commissioner of Scheduled Castes and Scheduled Tribes[31] in his report of the year 1970-71 (Appendix B) states :

"Even among Scheduled Castes and Scheduled Tribes, there are poorer and still poorer sections, neglected and even more neglected sections. It is therefore, the foremost duty of all concerned to ensure that these weaker sections, who, in fact, form the "weakest link" among the...Scheduled Tribes are located and given special attention for their development through specific programmes, undertaken for their uplift, based on their felt needs". The Commissioner puts the Korwa in the list of 'most backward' among the Scheduled Tribes in States of Madhya Pradesh and Bihar. Our purpose was to record facts of life of the people particularly those who are less known. The Hill Korwa, have not received much attention from anthropologists, sociologists and administrators."

(b) The Hill Korwa of Chattisgarh were selected with a view to undertaking a study in the area of their highest concentration.

(c) The Korwa are mainly divided into two groups : the Pahari or Hill Korwa and the Dehari/Dih or Plain dwelling Korwa. One can find a clear distinction between the two endogamous sub-groups while the former were shifting cultivators, till recently the latter are settled agriculturists.

(d) The Hill Korwa, as already stated, were shifting cultivators in their recent past. Shifting cultivation was banned by the Government of Madhya Pradesh with a view to protecting forest wealth. This caused a series of changes in the Korwa economy. An attempt to study the trends of change and connected problems confronting the people caused by abolition of slash and burn cultivation will be of some use for those who are responsible for upliftment of the weakest segments of society, such as the Hill Korwa as envisaged by the Commissioner of Scheduled Castes and Scheduled Tribes.

In the present study the author attempts to show the Korwa economy as it stands today. Shifting cultivation or *beora* is now almost a forgotten story. Due to abolition of *beora*, the Hill Korwa were forced to enter into the stage of settled agriculture. Agriculture presupposes the development of a different economic mechanism though largely under the control of 'market' or 'monetary economy', hunting and food gathering still contribute substantially to the Korwa livelihood.

The author will also endeavour to show that application of formal economic models is not useful to deal with the Hill Korwa, a 'non-market' or 'peripheral market' society.

In fact, the Korwa society has passed from one economic system based on food gathering and shifting cultivation to another economic system based on settled agriculture and is on the threshold of joining the forces of national economy based on market. The society has been subjected to various types of spontaneous and as well as planned changes.

The terms 'Hill Korwa' and 'Korwa' have appeared simultaneously in this report. Since this study deals specifically with the Hill Korwa, hence the term 'Korwa' should be taken as a synonym for the 'Hill' Korwa'.

METHODS OF STUDY

Selection of Villages

The field work for this study was done in two phases. In the first phase, one village in North-east Surguja was studied intensively for a period of six months. This investigator also took an extensive tour of the area and visited 27 villages inhabited by the Hill Korwa. In the second phase of work, two other villages, one from Surguja and the other from Raigarh district of Chhatisgarh region were selected for intensive study.

All four villages were selected in view of their predominant Korwa population. These villages were far from urban centres, thus the forces of acculturation were minimum and the traditional Korwa culture remained relatively undisturbed. All the four villages were situated in the deep forest seven to eighteen kilometres away from the road side. As this was the intention to bring into relief the core pattern of the Korwa culture exposed villages were purposely avoided.

The villages intensively studied are :

Village	*Tahsil*	*District*
a) Rakaiya	Samri	Surguja
b) Maltipur	Ambikapur	Surguja
c) Bansajhal	Ambikapur	Surguja
d) Sardapath	Jashpur	Raigarh

Rakaiya is situated in the north-east Surguja, below the Jonkapath hills. It had a homogeneous Hill Korwa population. In further north, the ethnic composition changes, the Korwa population gradually thins out and Kodaku population increases. In Jonkapath and Lehsunpath and the adjoining spur above Jonkapath, the proportion of the Korwa and Kodaku populations is more or less equal.

Maltipur is situated in the south-west Surguja on Mainpath Hills. Here, the Hill Korwa live side by side with the Nagesia and Oraons.Maltipur provided a chance to study the socio-economic relationships of the Hill Korwa with other tribes living in the village and also their relations with the Korwa living in the adjoining district of Bilaspur. The Oraon in this area have come under the influence of Christian missionaries. Hence this village was considered important to study the impact of Christian missionaries on the life of the Hill Korwa.

Bansajhal, is situated in the south-east Surguja adjoining Raigarh district. The village is multi-ethnic consisting of the *Mahto* (Ahir,) a dominant caste of the area and tribes viz., Oraon and Nagesia. It is the last Hill Korwa village in Surguja district in the south east direction.

Sardapath is situated in Khudia Zamidari of Raigarh district. Khudia Zamidar had a Dewan belonging to the Korwa tribe and a temple of Khudia Rani at Sanna, from where the Zamidari derived its name. All the Hill Korwa in Surguja claim their origin from Khudia. It is from here that the Hill Korwa spread throughout Chattisgarh. This village provided an opportunity to study the traditional political system of the Hill Korwa and also to draw a comparison between the Hill Korwa of Khudia, [which is supposed to be a place to which the Hill Korwa belong originally] with the Hill Korwa of Bansajhal, Maltipur and Rakaiya.

Establishing Rapport

In the initial stages of ethnographical research, an investigator is confronted with the problem of establishing a closer relationship with the people. This objective cannot be achieved without coming in close contact with the people. The initial difficulties faced by an investigator are in reaching to the people and convincing them about the earnestness of his purposes.

This author was warned both by tribals (other than Hill Korwa) and non-tribals that the Hill Korwa are difficult people and the area they inhabit is difficult to reach. They were reported as shy of outsiders and always under the influence of liquor. The author was told that if disturbed, they turn violent and take resort to killing at the slightest pretext. A high district official who had gone to a Korwa village in Raigarh District in connection with the recovery of loan from a Hill Korwa narrated his experiences in the following words :

"Hill Korwa are very bad people. Once they wanted to kill me. But for the presence of my *Sipahis*, I would have been killed".

The officials of the Tribal Development Blocks in respective areas were approached at the initial stage of the study for co-operation. The Hill Korwa have come into contact with the T.D. Blocks and became relatively frank with the block officials. The heads of traditional village council (*Mukhya*) of respective villages were summoned at respetcive block headquarters whom the author met and expressed his desire to stay with them in order to see what were their ways of life and how they faced their problems. This author showed them printed books and photographs of fellow tribals and expressed his desire to write a similar account on them. The heads of various Korwa Panchayats returned somewhat satisfied although they did not show any sign of enthusiasm in inviting a stranger amidst themselves. No sooner the author reached selected villages, called the elders, and explained his purpose through an interpreter picked out from amongst them, the heads of the respective villages, who had already met him earlier, extended support and co-operation and introduced him to other villagers.

The author invited the boys and girls of the villages to organise a dance performance, something dearest to a Korwa heart. The response was spontaneous. The participants and audience were entertained with sweets, cigarettes and other gifts. The following days marked the presence of a number of curious onlookers of all ages coming to the camp. They too were presented with small gifts. Rubber balls won the children's hearts and for coloured ribbon the Korwa girls went crazy. A transistorised radio set was a hit among village lads who would swarm the camp in the evenings after finishing their daily chores. Group interviews followed in packed evening sessions.

The field work started with door-to-door household census enumeration. All households of the village were numbered and a rough plan for each village was drawn showing houses and their respective numbers.

Interviews were held both with groups as well as with individuals. The group interviews dealt with the problems of general nature while interviews with individuals.

After establishment of a close liaison with the people the task of participant-observation appeared easy. The author had shown keen interest even in most ordinary aspect of the Korwa life and assumed some unimportant roles in their various rituals and hunting expeditions. He memorised some of their incantations (*mantras*) by-heart and acted once as one of the disciples of the priest and received a chicken as his reward. In hunting expeditions he assumed the role of a shouter. As the work progressed, he established putative kinship relationship with members of both the sexes and sometime offered them small gifts. In certain cases he was able to negotiate marriages between parties and participated from either of the sides as per demands of the situation.

Detailed genealogies were collected in order to understand and observe behaviour patterns of a group of kin at various ceremonies : quarrelling, joking, discussing, and behaving with one another in the light of their respective relationships. They could be located through genealogies. Thus the author could demonstrate that he was not a casual onlooker but he was deeply interested in each individual of the community as a sincere friend.

A few case studies bearing implications of various dimensions of socio-economic life of the people have also been collected in order to put the data in their real perspectives. These case situdies helped to bring out some of unnoticted aspects of the Korwa culture which were later probed for further details.

ECONOMIC ORGANIZATION OF
THE HILL KORWAS OF CHHATTISGARH
STUDY AREA

Based on the National Atlas of India

The Area

The Hill Korwa live near the trijunction of Madhay Pradesh, Bihar and Uttar Pradesh, while the majority of the Hill Korwa inhabit Surguja and Raigarh districts of Madhya Pradesh, fragments of them are found in the adjoining states of Bihar and Uttar Pradesh.

The field work on which the present account is based was carried out in the districts of Surguja and Raigarh, Madhya Pradesh.

Surguja

Surguja is one of recent districts of the State in the sense that it was constituted in the year 1951 consequent upon the merger of the erstwhile feudatory states of Surguja, Korea and Chang Bakhor. The etymology of the term Surguja is somewhat obscure, though according to some local scholars, the term is derived from two words : *sur* (god) and *gunja* (abode), 'Land where Gods lived'.[32] In support of their view they relate numerous stories, linking the area with the epic Ramyana. Although the historicity of such narrations remains questionable, there are evidences of early Hindu rule in the area.

There is no place in the district by the name Surguja. The district headquarter is situated at Ambikapur. Surguja is the second largest district in Madhya Pradesh in respect of area and is situated in the north-eastern corner of the state between latitude 22° 39′ and 24° 6′ N and longitude 81° 35′ and 84° 51′ E. The maximum width of the district from east to west is about 152 miles and the maximum length from north to south is about 104 miles. The total areas is 8,626 Sq. miles.

This district is bounded on the north by Mirzapur (U.P.) and Sidhi (M.P.) districts, on the east by Palamau district of Bihar on the south by Raigarh and Bilaspur districts of Madhya Pradesh and on the west by Shahdol district of the same state. In its general contour on the map, the district looks like the skull of a fox with its mouth towards the west.[33]

Geography

Physiographically Surguja and Raigarh districts are great table-lands consisting of numerous hills and plateaus. Except a low-lying basin in south-central region, the entire district of Surguja is a continuous stretch of plateau dotted with hills. The eastern part of the district consists of undulating table-land about 2500 feet high and continuous. It is slightly higher than Chotanagpur plateau. From this table-land, isolated hill ranges and the physiographic formations locally known as *path* rise to the elevation between 3,500 and 4,000 feet, forming the northern boundary with the Palamau district and blending on the south with the hill system of Jashpur tract of Raigarh District.

The higher peaks in the district range between 4,024 feet (Mailan) and 3027 feet (Murargarh). Others are between 2,000 and 3,000 feet in elevation.

The principal rivers of the district are Kanhar, the Geur, the Gaserd, the Gopath and the Neur besides Haddo and Gej in the south.

Raigarh

Raigarh district can be divided into two more or less well marked divisions. Latitude 22° 25′ which roughly demarcates the boundary between the northern hilly region and the southern plain may also be referred to as a 'watershed of ethnic groups'. To the north of this latitude one sees the ethnic types akin to that of the Chotanagpur plateau and represented by the Oraon, Korwa, Kharia, Nagesia, Majhwar, and Bhuihar and the south of the line is represented in the ethnic types close to that of the Chattisgarh and the plain region of Orissa, viz., Savara, Binjhwar, Gond, Painka, Teli, Satnami, and Kewat. Who are the autochthones of these tract is difficult to ascertain.[34]

The total population of the Korwa in Raigarh according to 1961 census figures is 19,010. They constitute 3.9 per cent of Scheduled Tribe population in the district. They have increased to 50.3 per cent since 1931 and are concentrated in Jashpur and Udaipur Tahsils. According to Dalton [35] "the typical Korwa inhabits the table-land Khuria in adjoining Jashpur Tahsil of Raigarh district".

Climate and Rainfall

The Districts of Surguja and Raigarh are generally cool, and heat even during the peak summer months, is not oppressive. May is the hottest month and December the coldest. The maximum temperature in May ranges from 39° C to 25.5° C.

They lie in the heavy rainfall area of the state and the average rain fall exceeds 55″. In the hilly and wooded region the rain fall is more copious.

Flora

The two districts lie in the *Sal* forest belt. The Sal is locally known as Sakhua (Shorea robusta). *Asan* (Terminalia tomentosa), *Dhauwara* (Anogessuslatifolia), *Tendu* (Terminalia belerica), *Harra* (Terminalia Chebula) *Char* (Buchanania latifolia), *Khair* (Acacia catechu), *Kauha* (Terminalia arjuna), Palas (Butea frondosa), Kusum (Schleichera trisuga), are other species usually found there.

During the erstwhile feudatory Estates' regime in Surguja and Raigarh large blocks of forest areas were kept reserved for the respective chiefs as hunting grounds.

Fauna

Abul Fazl Allami[36] mentions in his Chronicle Ain-e-Akbari that 'elephants are found......in the confines of Surguja'. Hence it is evident that the district was the home of wild elephants in the past. There are no wild elephants in Surguja now. Bison and wild Buffaloes too have become very scarce. Tigers (Felis tigris), panthers (Felis parodus) and bears (Malasus) are commonly met within the forest and hill areas. Other common wild animals are sambhar (Cervus unicolom) Nilgai (Bos-Elephas tragocamelus), ravine deer (Gazella bennethi), Hog Deer and Mouse Deer.

History

The early history of the two districts is somewhat obscure. Although District Census Handbook, Surguja mentions that this tract appears to have been unknown to the Moghul Government, Abul Fazl does make a mention of Surguja in *Ain-e- Akbari*. From the remains of extensive rock excavations supposed to be temples and monastries discovered in Harchoka village of Bharatpur Tehsil it appears probable that in early times, the district was occupied by a civilized race. Who the people were and what was their period of stay is however, unknown (D.C.H. Surguja : XII).

In 1758 a Maratha army overran the eastern half of the district and compelled the chief to acknowledge himself as a tributary of the Berar Government. Beyond this, the Marathas did not take interest in the affairs of Surguja. In 1792, the three erstwhile feudatory states which constitute the present district ceded to the British Government. The British force appointed Amar Singh as the Chief of Surguja. Amar Singh's rule lasted till 1852. On his death his eldest son Indrajit Singh succeeded to the throne in 1853. Indrajit Singh died in 1897 and his son Raghu Nath Singh was declared the ruler of Surguja. He ruled Surguja till his death in 1917. After his death Maharaja Ramanuj Sharan Singh came to the throne and ruled the state tlll 1942. The last Maharaja adopted modern techniques of administration and contradicted by his rule the old saying, 'mare-na-jahur Khai, chalat chalat Surguja jai' i.e. one need not take poison to die (if one wishes so) but should walk into Surguja. The implicit meaning of the above proverb suggests that in the past whosoever dared to enter in Surguja was either killed by tigers or by the Hill Korwas or Kodakus. The new Maharaja himself killed many tigers during various hunting expeditions and imposed heavy penalties on the Korwas and Kodakus. He made the Korwa chiefs responsible to control their people and granted them allowances and red-turbans.[37]

Density of Population

Notwithstanding the high growth of populations, Surguja is the second most sparsely populated district in the state and the number of persons per square mile is 122 against 194 for the division and 190 for the state. The tehsilwise density of population in 1951 and 1961 of Ambikapur and Samri Tehsils is 150, 190 and 95, 119 respectively.

Scheduled Castes and Scheduled Tribes

Surguja is the fourth biggest district in the state in respect of proportion of Scheduled Tribes. According to the Census, 1961 nearly 56 per cent of its population belong to Scheduled

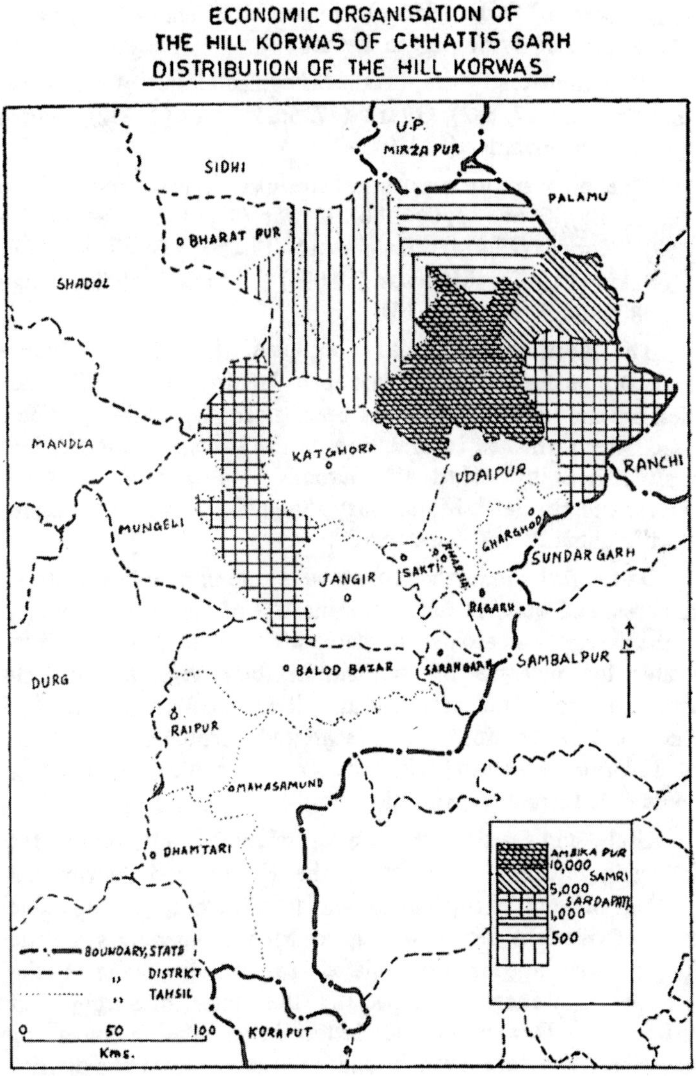
ECONOMIC ORGANISATION OF
THE HILL KORWAS OF CHHATTIS GARH
DISTRIBUTION OF THE HILL KORWAS
U.P.
MIRZA PUR
SIDHI
PALAMU
BHARAT PUR
SHADOL
MANDLA
KATGHORA
UDAIPUR
RANCHI
MUNGELI
GHARGHODA
SUNDAR GARH
JANGIR
SAKTI
RAGARH
BALOD BAZAR
SARANGARH
SAMBALPUR
N
DURG
RAIPUR
MAHASAMUND
DHAMTARI
AMBIKA PUR
10,000
SAMRI
5,000
SARDAPUR
1,000
500
BOUNDARY, STATE
DISTRICT
TAHSIL
0
50
100
Kms.
KORAPUT

Tribes. As per Scheduled Castes and Scheduled Tribes Lists (modification) Order 1956, there are 15 Scheduled Castes and 32 Scheduled Tribes in the district

The numerically important Scheduled Castes of the district are Chamar (27, 882), Ghasia (17, 562), Basor (4, 632), Chikwa (3,358)and Rohidas (1, 119).

The numerically important Scheduled Tribes are the Gond (2, 22, 278), Oraon (1, 06, 186), Kawar (92, 132), Nagesia (28, 127), Korwa (20,414), Kahairwar (19,460), Pando (18,707), Kodaku (14,768), Majhwar (10,096), Agaria (9,552), Baiga (7, 480) and Bhuihar (7,713).

The Korwa appear to have occupied the minds of rulers and administrators for the last one hundred years. The earliest account of the Korwa has been given by Dalton, others who have furnished information on the Korwas are Risley and Gait[38], De Brett[39], Hutton[40], Crooks[41], Bhaduri[42], Driver[43], Russel and Hiralal[44], Majumdar[45], Singh[46], Prasad[47] and Bhandari[48], Ahmad[49] and Sandhwar[50].

Dalton feels that thc Korwa were the first inhabitants of the area and were at one time masters of the whole country ...the savage and alomst nomadic life they lead is not favourable for increase of population...they were at one time more numerous and powerful and it is possible that many of the broken tribes now found scattered throughout this part of India once formed with the Korwa people united under some rude form of Government.

Risely and Gait[51] in the Census of India 1901, furnish the following information regarding the Korwa and distribution of their population in Central India: "The only considerable tribe of Western Bengal who speak Munda languages are the Korwa...who appear to be related to Mundas, inhabit the West of Chotanagpur especially the states of Surguja and Jashpur, the Dewan of the latter being the member of the trIbe. They are even found in that part of the district of Mirzapur which lies South of the Son (river), being the only Munda tribe speaking a Munda language in the United Provinces. Here, their language is called Korwari, Singli and Ernga are said to be the dialect of Korwari.

De Brett[52] in the beginning of twentieth century depicts the Korwa in the following words:

"The Korwas are liable to outbreaks of crime, which usually take the form of an attack on an Ahir, a class of men, who by their reckless manner in which they allow their cattle to damage the cultivations of these aborigines, often excite the latter to reprisals. Occasionally they also attack the passing traders to get salt or cloth, or a liquor shop to get a supply of drink. These men are usually armed with bows and arrows, spears and axes and since they do not hesitate to use their weapons and are usually in considerable force, they are formidable opponents to unarmed people".

Risley, Hutton, Crooks, Driver, Russel and Hira Lal and Prasad have made only passing reference to the Hill Korwa. Thus, their accounts shed little light on the life and culture of the people. Majumdar did field work among the Korwa in the trijunction of Mirzapur, Surguja and Palamu. Bhandari has studied Kinship organization of the Korwa of Mirzapur (U.P.) only. Prasad's brief account of the people is based on the Korwa of Palamu (Bihar) and Singh has made a brief mention of Korwa while bringing into relief the past and present of the Surguja District. His accounts are based more on hearsay than any genuine field work. Ahmad has mainly dwelt upon the physical aspect of the Hill Korwa of Surguja. Sandhwar discusses the impact of Christian missionaries on the Korwa of Palamu.

None of the above mentioned studies have dealt with the social economy of the Hill Korwa with considerable depth. Dalton however, has dealt with the Korwa life in general and brings into relief some important historical fact about the origin of the people and distribution of their population in the last phase of the nineteenth century A.D.

Origin of the People

According to Captain Samuels, Assistant Commissioner quoted by Dalton[53] "the first human being settled in Surguja was very much troubled by the depredations of wild beasts on their crops. He put up scare-crow in his field, figures made of bamboos dangling in the air to frighten the animals".

"When the 'great spirit' saw the scare crow he hit on an expedient his trouble of reconstructing them. He animated the dangling figures, thus bringing into existence creatures ugly enough to frighten the birds and beasts...and they were the ancestors of the Hill Korwa.

In Rakaiya, the Hill Korwa narrated to this author the following story of their origin:

A scare-crow (*druna*) holding a bow and arrow was installed to frighten birds (viz. *pandki*) Rama's wife (Sita) asked her husband to animate the figure. Rama asked Sita "What for I should give a new soul to it"? (thinking it is something insignificant). Rama's wife replied, "If you do not animate the scare-crow (*druna*) I will cease living with you, and will request you to pass your life the way you like and I will be passing mine (separately)". Hearing this Rama conceded to his wishes animated the figure and transformed it into a human figure holding a bow and arrow. He was the first Korwa from whom the present Korwa came into being and never parted with a bow and since then".

In Sardapath (Raigarh), the Hill Korwa gave the version similar to the above story excepting the variation that instead of 'Rama and his wife', they held Sankar and Parvati responsible for animating the scare-crow. The above versions differ only on the point as to who animated the scare-crow whether the 'great spirit' (Dalton), Rama and his wife (Rakaiya), or Sankar and Parvati (Sardapath).

A different verion regarding the origin of the people was given by Sri A.L. Dubey (the then Deputy Director, Social Welfare, M.P. Government (Personal Communication). It runs as follows:

"Parvati had two sons. Once both of them were sitting on her lap (*kor*). One of them fled from there and the other remained sitting thereon. One who fled from the Parvati's lap (*kor*) was called Kodaku and one who remained sitting in her lap was named Korwa". The Korwa informants did not lend support to this story.

The Place of Origin

A consensus among all Korwa informants was that the place of their origin was Khuria in Jaspur Tahsil of Raigarh District. The area under the erstwhile Khuria Zamindari is treated as a Scheduled Area specified in Scheduled Area (Part A-States) orders, 1950, Census of India.

We find the following description of the erst-while Khuria Zamindari furnished by Dalton (ibid).[54]

"The present Raja of Jashpur fully admits that the Korwa Dewan's ancestors were the original rulers of the country. His own family counts only seventeen generations since assuming the throne, and were first established in the low-lands where the remains of their ancient strongholds may still be seen. They were Khairwars, whom, I suppose to have been an off-shoot of the same race and their tradition that they were driven out of Belonja in Bihar may refer to the break of the Chero-Kol-Khairwar nation formerly located in Magadh. The family having established themselves in the low-lands gradually brought the high landers under subjection, but the great high land chief only yielded on condition that he was to be acknowledged as the second person in realm, the lieutenant or Dewan. This was conceded and from generations there was no breach of the contract till the grandfather of the present Raja, disregarding the ancient policy of his family confided the affairs of the Raj to his foster-brother a Kahar named Anant Ram. The hereditary Korwa Dihan Munawar Singh, resented this and a small war ensued which lasted for many years and was still in active operation when Jashpur with Surguja and other territories ceded to the British Government by Appa Sahib. Some of the Government troops were sent to co-operate with the Raja against his refractory vassal but they made very little impression on the Korwas, and Munawar Singh fought till he died in A.D. 1821.

"His son Maniar Singh, who has been captured during the hostilities and under the guarantee of the British Government was reinstated with all the hereditary honours and possessions of the family, since when the Jashpur Korwas have always conducted themselves peacably and loyally."

"There were in existence within the last twenty years as highlanders, chiefs and holders of manors four Korwa notables, two in Surguja and two in Jashpur; all four estates were valuable as they comprised substantial villages in the fertile plains and great tracts of hilly country on which were scattered the hamlets of their more savage followers. The Surguja Korwa chiefs were, however, continually at strife with the Surguja Raja and for various acts of rebellion against Lord Paramount, lost manor after manor till each but one or two villages remained.

This was the position when the mutiny of 1857 broke out and like many others, they thought the disturbances and anarchy that supervened afforded them an opportunity of recovering what they had lost. Placing themselves at the head of their clansman, they committed a series of raids on the low-land villages and whole-sale plundering and murdering were restored to for a time but ere long the insurrection was cut short by capture of two chiefs: one of them who was convicted for murder was hanged the other was amnestied and died.

The two Jashpur thanes conducted themselves right loyally at this crucial period and they are now prosperous gentlemen in the full enjoyment of their estates...one of them is the hereditary Dewan of Jashpur, lord of the whole tribe of Korwas. The other holds as estate called Kakia, comprising twenty two villages in the low-land and some hill country.

It can be derived from the above account that the Korwa of Jashpur were actual rulers of the land till the middle of fourteenth century. They were latter subjugated by the Kharwar rulers. The Dewanship was granted to Korwa high landers. This system remained in practice till the beginning of the nineteenth century. In the second decade of nineteenth century there were clashes between the Raja and the Korwa Dewan. This perhaps attracted Britishers and the State of Jashpur was ceded to them in 1818".

Language

The Hill Korwa of Surguja speak a dialect known as Korwari which is closely related to Mundari. They are gradually abandoning their old dialect which has been replaced by Kurukh. The Chattisgarhi spoken by Hill ,.Korwa in Jashpur tract is known as Sadri Korwa.[55]

The present author has quoted Dalton copiously as he feels that the detailed accounts of Dalton are helpful in lifting the curtain from the hazy past of the people and to provide a pase line for studying changes that occurred in the society, during the last one hundred years.

REFERENCES

1. Marshal, A. 1936. *Principles of Economics*, 8th Edition, London.
2. Danda, A.K. 1977. 'Tribal Economy of Chattisgarh, in *Chattisgarh : An Area Study*. Ed. by A.K. Danda, Calcutta, Anthropological Survey of India.
3. Polanyi, Karl., et al. 1957. *Trade and Market in Early Empires* Glencoe. Illinois, Free Press.
4. Polanyi, Karl., 1957. ibid 3
5. Dalton. 1969. "Theoretical issues in Economic Anthropology". *Current Anthropology*, 1 : 63-102.
6. Lewis, Arthur W. 1962. 'Foreword' in *Economic Development and Social Change in South India* by T. Scarlett Epstein. Manchester : University Press.
7. Firth, Raymond. 1958. *The Element of Social Organization*. Lodon Watts and Co.
8. Barnett, H.G. 1968. "Making Money" in *Economic Anthropology Readings in Theory and Analysis*. Ed. by Edward E. Le Clair, Jr. and Harold K. Schneider, New York : Holt Rinehart.

9. Epstein Scarlett 1967. "Productive Efficiency and customary systems of rewards in rural South India" in *Themes in Economic Anthropology*, Ed. by Raymond Firth. London. Tavistock : 229-252.

10. Samuelson, Paul A. 1964. *Economics : An Introductory Analysis*. New York :Mc Graw Hills.

11. Cook, Scott. 1966. "The obsolete Antimarket mentality : A critique of substantive approach" in *American Anthropologist*, 68, 1.

12. Le Clair, Edward E. 1962. "Economic theory and Economic Anthropology" in *American Anthropologist* 64 : 1179-1203.

13. Nash, Manning. 1961. "The social content of economic choice in a small society" in *Man*, LIX : 186-91.

14. Panoff, Michel, 1970. "Marcel Mauss's The Gift Revisited" in *Man*, 5 (1) : 60-70.

15. Bennet, John W. 1968. "Reciprocal Economic Exchanges among North American Agricultural operators" in *Southwestern Journal of Anthropology* : 24 (3) 276-309.

16. Kaplan, David. 1968. "The Formal-substantive controversy in Economic Anthropology : Reflections on its wider implications" in *Southwestern Journal of Anthropology* 24 (3), 228-51.

17. Bailey, F.G. 1969. "Capital, Saving and Credit in Highland Orissa (India)" in *Capital, Saving and Credit in Peasant Societies* Ed. by Raymond Firth and B.S. Yamey. London. George Allen and Unwin : 105-132.

18. Danda, A.K. ibid : 2

19. Roy, S.C. 1915. *The Oraons of Chota Nagpur*, Ranchi.

20. Majumdar, D.N. 1930. "The Economic background of social institution in Primitive Socities" in *Man in India* 10 : 150-66.

21. Dutta Majumdar, 1940. The Economic Organization of the Bhotia.

22. Chattopadhyaya, K.P. 1947. Economic condition of the Korkus of Melghat Forest in *Journal of Royal Asiatic Society of Bengal*, XII (1) : 19-30.

23. Dube, S.C., 1947. "The Economic Life of Kamar" in *Man in India*, XXVII (2) : 137-169.

24. Haimendorf, Von-Furer. 1949. Seasonal Nomadism and Economics of Chenchus of Hyderabad in *Journal of Royal Asiatic Society of Bengal*. VI : 175-196.

25. Husain. S. Khaja Mehboob. 1949. "The rural uplift of tribe and backward classes in Hyderabad Deccan" in *Man in India*, XXIX (3) and (4) : 185-198.

26. Apte, J.S. 1960. "Co-operative Movement among the Tribes of Thana, Bombay State" in *Vanyajati*, VIII (3) : 102-104.

27. Nag, D.S. 1958. *Tribal Economy*, Delhi, Bhartiya Admjati Sevak Sangh.

28. Mukhejee, B. 1955. "Riang Economy" in *Bulletin of Anthropological Survey of India*. Calcutta IV (2).

28. A. Singh, K.S. 1982. *Economics of the Tribes and their Transformation* Ed. KS. Singh

29. Report of Commissioner of Scheduled Castes and Scheduled Tribes :1968-69.

30. Danda, A.K. ibid : 2

31. Report of Commissioner of Scheduled Castes Scheduled Tribes : 1970-71 (Appendix-B).

32. District Census Handbook, Surguja District (M.P.), 1964, Census of India, 1961.

33. District Census Handbook, Raigarh District (M.P.), 1964, Census of India 1961.

34. Dalton, E.T. 1872. *Descriptive Ethnology of Bengal*, Calcutta. Mukhopadhyaya : 220-228.

35. Op cit.

36. Allami, Abul Fazl. 1594. *Ain-e-Akbari* (Persian). Translated by H. Blochman. Delhi : 129: 129.

37. Singhdeo, Samar Bahadur. 1957. *Surguja Ka Ek Adhyayan* (Hindi). Ambikapur ; 50.

38. Gait, E.P. and H.H. Risley, 1901. *Census of India* 1, Part I, Report : 415.

39. de Brett, E.A. 1909. Chattisgarh Feudatory Gazetteer. Bombay, Times Press :233-236.

40. Hutton, J.H. 1946. *Caste in India* (Glossary). London, Oxford University Press, 80.

41. Crooks, W. 1892. "A vocabulary of Korwa Language' in *Journal of Asiatic Society of Bengal*, LX, 1 : 125.

42. Bhaduri, M.B. 1937. "The Korwas of Udaipur State (C.P.)" in *Man in India*, 17, 127-46.

43. Driver, W.H.P. 1891. "Notes on some Kolarian Tribes" in *Journal of Royal Asiatic Society of Bengal*, LXI, Part I : 14.

44. Russel, R.V. and R.B. Hira Lal, 1916. *The Tribes aud Castes of Central* India, Vol. XIV. London, Macmillan.

45. Majumdar, D.N. 1944. *Fortunes of Primitive Tribes*, Lucknow, Universal Publishers, Ltd.

46. Singhdeao, Samar Bhadur. ibid : 18

47. Prasad, N. 1961. "Korwa" in *Land and People of Tribal Bihar*, Ranchi ; 193-96.

48. Bhandari, J.S. 1963. "Kinship, Family and Marriage among the Korwas of Dudhi"; in *Eastern Anthropologist*. 16 (2) : 79-106.

49. Ahmad, S. S.H. 1973. "Anthropometric Measurements of the Korwas of Surguja" in *Eastern-Anthropologist*. 16 (2) : 79-106.

50. Sandhwar. 1973. "The method of Christian conversion among the Tribes: The Korwa converts of Palamu-A case study". *Journal of Social Research*.

51. Risley Gait ibid : 28

52. de Brett. ibid : 28

53. Dalton. op cit. 23

54. Dalton. ibid : 23

55. Grierson, G.A. 1967. *Linguistic Survey of India*, IV, 147-151.

CHAPATER TWO

The People

Material Culture

The study of various aspects of material life of the Korwa is important not only from the basic interests of the artifacts themselves, but also for knowing their sources of origin and channels of diffusion. Further, artifacts and associated techniques have great importance because of their relationship with the entire socio-economic and religious fabric of Korwa life.

Dwelling

The Korwa dwellings are of two types : a) Permanent and b) Temporary.

An average Permanent dwelling consists of two rooms measuring approximately 8 × 10 feet attached invariably with a cattleshed and a verandah. A small kitchen garden is also raised with the dwelling.

A rough plan of a Korwa household as found in Rakaiya is shown on page 30.

On one side of the Verandah is kept the grinding stone (G.S. *janta*). Husking level (H.L.) or *dhanki* is placed on the other side. Room 1 is meant for sitting-cum-sleeping purpose. At one corner of a room the hearth (H) *chulha* is placed.

On the right side of the wall a shelf (s) is put for keeping clothes, artifacts, and other household goods.

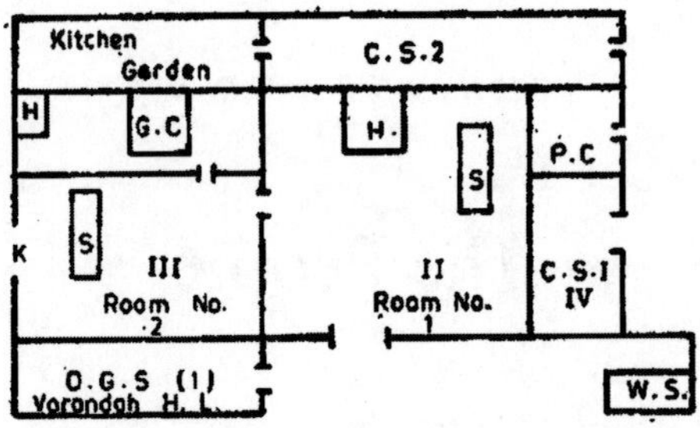

Diagram 2.1 : Plan of a Korwa House

Room 2 is ordinarily used for sleeping-cum-storing where grain containers (G.C.), musical instruments, and pots of brewing *handi* are kept. Arrows, bows, and axes hang from the wall. Sickles, rolls of mat both finished and unfinished are kept besides a number of broom sticks. The family deities (*bhitardeo*) is also placed in this room.

Cattleshed (C.S.) are of two types. In C.S. 1 bullocks and cows are kept while in C.S. 2 goats are kept. A poultry cage is generally attached with C.S. 2. Those possessing pigs use C.S. 2 as pigsty also. Kitchen garden is attached with C.S. 2 with an outlet for throwing manure in the kitchen garden. On the backwall of Room 2 there is a small window, most of the time covered with leaves and twigs (K). It is used as the entrance of menstruating and pregnant women who are otherwise forbidden to enter in to the house from the main entrance in their state of pollution.

Temporary huts are known as *koomba*. It is conical in shape and erected on a plot of land circumference of which does not usually go beyond six feet. It is erected mainly for aged widowers or widows who sleep therein with small children. *Koombas* are also erected under *mahua* trees during flowering season to facilitate picking up *mahua* flowers. The watch huts to ward off burglers, beasts, and birds are also of this type.

Wood, mud, straw, leaves, and twigs are the materials by which a Korwa house is built. The walls are made by putting wooden logs vertically at regular gap of six inches. These gaps are filled in by putting transversed logs horizontally at a distance of one inch. The wall is further reinforced by putting twigs all around. When the structure is ready, it is plastered with mud. Three beams are pitched on the ground to lend support to a horizontal beam. A number of beams extend from the central beam toward the walls above tne ground. Transverse wooden beams are now put to complete the structure of the roof which is thatched by straw.

During the last five decades a change has occurred in the Korwa architecture. These days baked tiles are used for thatching the roof. These tiles were first brought by the neo-settlers from Bihar and Uttar Pradesh. With the introduction of baked tiles the walls have better protection against rain water. Now the Korwa prefer simple mud wall to the old system of erecting wall by pitching poles.

The raw materials needed for construction of a Korwa house are locally available. The Hill Korwa have also learnt the art of moulding roof tiles and baking them on slow heat. Wood, required for structure of a house, is available in the forests and the people themselves make doors and window panels.

Construction of a house is purely a domestic affair. No labourers are engaged from outside for this purpose. If the number of household labourers is not sufficient, the members of the lineage concerned (*bhaiyar*) co-operate in house-building activities. In return, they are entertained with food and home-made beer (*handi*).

The settlement pattern in a Korwa village is dispersed as the houses are mostly situated near their respective agricultural fields. This pattern seems to be a carryover of the past. When the people were shifting cultivators, they used to erect dwellings beside their agricultural fields and move out to another site after harvesting was over. After abolition of the practice of shifting cultivation the Hill Korwa were rehabilitated in forest villages. They were asked to live in the houses built in clusters. Rakaiya was one such village where 15 houses were built in two parallel rows in the year 1954. After 15 years, the number of households increased to 31 . The new houses that have been constructed during these past 15 years were again scattered and dispersed. Now, Rakaiya presents a settlement pattern of scattered type. In the year 1970, some of Government Officials alleged that the Hill Korwa commit thefts and conceal the booty in their scattered houses. According to them it poses problems in recovering the stolen property. Hence the Hill Korwa have been asked to construct their houses in clusters.

Equipments and Implements

Equipments and implements of the Hill Korwa consist of bows, arrows, digging sticks, and axes of various types. The arrow heads are of two types : a) for killing the game and for stunning birds and rabits. The former variety is made of iron and known as *bissar*. They are made by the local ironsmiths. The other variety is *beetha*. An arrow consists of five parts 1) the arrow head, which is pointed at the top. The two cutting edges diverge from the point to make two fangs on either side of the arrow head. 2) The fangs are called *Kani*. (3) From the middle of the lower end of arrow-head in between the fangs emerge a pointed needle which is hafted into a piece of reed about 1/2 feet in length. (4) The piece of reed which is known as *tir* is hafted on one end with arrowhead and on the other with feathers of crow, vulture, or kite. At the feather-end of the arrow, a small grove is made in order to facilitate a firm grip with the bow-string. The reed is cut into pieces of desired length. Now, the pieces are straightened by smoking them on a slow fire. The feathers are attached by thong in order to provide balance to an arrow in its trajectory. The size of arrow heads varies according to their function. Smaller arrow heads measuring three to four inches are used to kill smaller games viz., fowls, rabbits and spotted deer while bigger arrow heads of about six inches length are used for boars, blue-bulls, and bears.

The bow is known as *dhanu*. It is made of bamboo and thong. The stave (*dhanu*) and string (*nam-dhin*) are made of bamboo. The string is attached to two arms of the bow by thong.

There are four types of axes. *Tangi* is a small axe having two types of cutting edges. In triangular shape, the cutting edges form the base of a triangle while the top of triangle is hafted into a wooden handle, *baint*. It the other type of the small axe, the cutting edge assumes a curvature as it is tapered towards the shaft fitted with a wooden handle. *Tabal* is a bigger axe. The cutting edge of its blade is a convex crescent and the two ends of the crescent form the shaft. The blade is decorated with floral designs. *Balua* also falls in the similar category. The cutting edge of the blade bears a depression in the middle and bulges at the side-ends. It is convex at the two sides of the blade and concave in the middle. The axes are mainly used for felling trees but they also serve as a weapon whenever a necessity arises.

Two types of fishing traps are found. One for fishing in shallow water and the other for deep water. The former is known as *mandra* and is made of bamboo strips tied with bark ropes. It is conical in shape. The upper end of the cone is about three inches in circumference while the lower end has a circumference of 15 inches. Bamboo strips edge out at the base of the cone. On one side of the trap, a handle (*tangna*) is attached. The total length of the implement is 30 inches.

The trap used for deep water fishing is known as *hata*. It is made of bamboo strips parabolic in shape. The bamboo strips extend from a parabolic rim and are interspersed with one another making small hole in the bottom of the trap. The implement is drowned in the water and then lifted up. The water filters down leaving fish in the trap. Two types of traps were found for trapping birds and hare, (a *Lassa phanda* and (b) *Kheencha phanda*. *Lassa phanda* is mainly used by childern. It consists of a bamboo container of about 10 inches long and one inch in circumference and a bundle of thin bamboo strips tied with cotton thread. Inside the bamboo container a paste of gum mixed with oil is kept into which the bamboo strips are immersed. The bamboo strips are thus coated with gum paste. These strips are put on branches of trees or in the grass and the gummed strips strick in feather or feet of an approaching bird rendering the latter unable to fly. Consequently the bird falls down and is captured alive.

Kheencha phanda trap used for trapping birds and hare is made of bamboo sticks and loops made of hair of horses or ponies. The bamboo sticks are fitted into many parallel and horizontal collapsable bamboo rods in a zig-zag manner, on both upper and lower ends making small rectangles and squares. A loop of hair suspends within each rectangle. The vertical bamboo rods are fastened to the ground and the loops keep hanging one inch above the ground. Small birds, fowls, peacocks, and hares are chased and pushed towards the traps. If the game wants to ıun through the hair loops latter becomes constricted making a noose by which the game cannot pass and falls down due to strangulation.

The above *Keencha phanda* was seen only in one village with one household of Sardapath and does not traditionally belong to the Hill Korwa but is being borrowed from other tribes.

Fishing and trapping are a subsidiary means of Korwa livelihood who put more emphasis on hunting by bows and arrows. The people dislike trapping of animals and birds which is devoid of the thrill, achievement, and pride. Hunting, on the contrary, is not only major source of Korwa livelihood but it provides them with the best entertainment. Even rats, which form one of the favourite dishes of the Hill Korwa, are not trapped but are usually given a chase before they are killed. If a mouse runs inside its burrow, a Korwa removes the entire amount of earth for capturing it alive.

The only implement which is a reminiscent of food gathering activities of the people is a dibble (*Chanti*) by which the people dig the soil and extract out roots and tubers.

Agricultural implements of the Hill Korwa consist of a plough (*har*) with iron share (*phar*), a yoke (*Juath*), leveller (*petla*) and sickles (*hansia*). The iron part of the implements are purchased from Lohars mostly in return of food-grains whereas the wooden parts of all implements are manufactured by the people themselves. Every Korwa family does not possess a pair of bullocks for ploughing purposes. Hence land is dug manually by help of a shovel (*pharsa*) which is made of a broad iron blade hafted into a wooden handle.

Dress and Adornment

Men wear a loin-cloth below the abdomen. On special occasions they cover the upper portion of the body with a single piece of thick cotton cloth. Women cover their lower portion of the body with an under garment (*kapuna*) around which a single piece of cloth is tied (*looga*) in the form of a a mini-skirt. The upper half portion of the cloth covers the upper portion of the body. Most of the clothes worn by the Hill Korwa are hand-woven and supplied by the Painka who visit Korwa villages and weekly markets regularly.

Ornaments are worn by both Korwa men and women. Men put on metallic bangles, mostly made of aluminium, bead necklaces and ear rings. Women put on silver necklaces (*hansli*) also. Their ear-plugs (*tarki*) are either made of wood or a roll of palm leaf. Glass studded wooden ear-plugs are also common. Bracelet made of alluminum are also worn by women. Ornaments are procured from the Malar. Silver ornaments are procured from Sunars but scarcely used.

Women use wooden combs (*kakkai*) for hair-dressing. Hair is tied into a knot over the occiput. A coloured cotton thread with a bunch of flowers (also made of coloured cotton) on both the ends, known as *phundna* is tied around the coiffure.

Hygiene and Cleanliness

Both men and women bath regularly. Men take bath in the afternoon after finishing the daily chores in the way-side ponds or nearby streams. Women wash their hair with yellowish clay (*mooner-matti*). No soaps or detergents are used by the peoples very few can afford to buy them. They know the indigenous cleansing agents. After the bath oil is anointed on the body and hair.

Clothes and utensils are cleaned by ash. Sometimes clothes are boiled in water and ash, and then washed in the nearby stream.

Personal hygiene and cleanliness are given a high importance. "He, who, remains dirty does not evoke Bhagwan's blessings" said Nadi Korwa of Rakaiya. None will participate in ritual without having a bath. Women during menstruation and child-birth are not allowed to cook or enter into the *bhitar-ghar* where family spirits are supposed to live. This may distrub the spirits which may cause harm to her and the family.

Unlike the neighbouring tribes, viz., the Kawar, Oraon, and Nagesia, Hill Korwa are marked with an absolute absence of tattooing which is avoided due to its high cost which they can hardly afford.

Food Habits

The staple diet of the Hill Korwa is millet. Rice and maize are luxury items. Chicken, mutton, and pork are consumed on special occasions. Fruits, leaves, flowers and tubers are important supplementary food items. Tomatoes, beans, papayas, gourds, pumpkins, and brinjals, chillies, radish and turnip are cultivated in tiny kitchen gardens. Games are rarely available but when captured are eaten with great relish. Eggs are scarcely eaten. They instead, prefer to increase the number of fowls. Milk is consumed, rarely as they generally leave milk for kids and calves. *Ghee* and butter are almost unknown to a Hill Korwa. *Kurthi* (Dolichos biflours) and *rahar* are used but rarely as pluses. Oil as a cooking medium is used by very few who can afford it. The Korwa meals are mostly boiled or baked. Parched maize (*lai*), millets, and sometimes black gram is taken as the afternoon refreshment.

Thr hearth (*chulha*) as stated earlier, is usually situated in the corner of the sitting-cum-bedroom. Each nuclear family unit owns a *chulha* of its own. The number of Chulhas in a household thus indicates the number of nuclear families, Wood is used as a fuel. Fire is kept burning round the clock. The art of fire-making by simple drill is knwn to the people but the easy availability of match boxes have put fire drills into disuse.

Millets are ground into flour by housewives in *janta* (hand-driven mill) and a hard dough is prepared from the flour. Small balls of the dough are given shape to thick circular cakes which are baked on slow fire or hot ashes. Millet cakes are sometimes sweetened by mixing a paste of *meehua* floweres or little amount of jaggery. Millets are dehusked, boiled, and eaten as a substitute of rice. Goats, pigs and chickens are cut into pieces and cooked in earthen pot. Salt and spices are added according to taste. Meals are served in leafy dishes (*dona*).

Fruits: Mango, guava, jack-fruit, and papaya are eaten both raw and ripe. Immatured jack-fruit is boiled with salt and green papaya (*mewa*) is cooked with chicken. Green mango is ground with salt and chillies and the paste is eaten with millet cakes. Leafy vegetables (mustard leaves, wild spinach, and gram leaves) are boiled with little quantity of salt and chillies according to taste and eaten with millet caes or boiled millets. Mahua (Bassia latifolia) flowers are eaten raw or boiled. Mahua fruits are sweet and highly relished by the people. Its seeds are pressed in wooden crusher (*patni*) for extracting oil which is used a cooking medium. Mahua trees are planted by the Korwa and carefully looked after. The owner of a mahua tree is considered fortunate by his kinsmen.

Tubers, which supplement the Korwa diet are pitharoo, saidoo, gaith, doodhia, and nakwa. Pitharoo, saidoo, and doodhia are eaten raw. Nakwa is boiled and eaten. Gaith needs a special processing before consumption because of its highly bitter and pungent taste. It is cut into pieces, boiled, and put in a container for 24 hours in the flowing stream. It is boiled for the second time and then eaten.

Ths Hill Korwa eat twice a day. The mid-day meal is known as *kelwa* which consists of millet cakes with a paste of vegetable or chutney. Boiled millets are eaten with pulses and leafy vegetables. The same articles are repeated in the evening meals (*biyari*) which is eaten after the sun set. In between *kalwa* and *biyari* parched maize, millet, or gram are taken as refreshment. The left-over food is eaten the next morning.

The Hill Korwa eat beef and carrion but certain species of birds and animals are avoided. No explanation could be obtained for the same. The following table lists the permissible and prohibited species of birds, animals and insects.

TABLE 2.1

Prohibited and Permissible Items of Korwa Food

	Birds	Animals	Reptiles/ Insects/ Fish
Prohibited	Vultures, Crow, Eagles, Kite	Jackal, Hyena, Horse, Dog, Cat, Monkey, Bear, Tiger	Snakes, Worms
ermissible	All available species excepting the above	Cow, Bullock, Buffalo, Pig, Dear, Hare of all varieties, Goat, Boar and Rat.	

Drinking water is fetched from shallow wells (*dhonri*) or natural streams. Natural water trickling from the rocks is collected by inseiting a piece of hollow bamboo in the hole from which water oozes out. This source of supply is irregular as the natural streams go dry during summer days.

Drinks and Narcotics

Handi is the traditional drink of the Hill Korwa. The drink which is prepared at home occupies an important place in all life-cycle rituals and forms an inseparable part of Korwa political organization, economy, and religion. Its supply indicates prosperity, leisure, and achievement. The cultural activities of the people revolves round the *handi.* It is prepared by fermenting millets and cooked rice. The drink which is prepared by fermenting mahua flowers is known as *jagra* and it is red in colour whereas *handi* is dim white. The Drink is enjoyed by all irrespective of age and sex. There are some unauthorised liquor shops (*gaddis*) in many villages of Suruguja and Raigarh. *Gaddis* are run by the tribals for which a commission is given to them by the *bhatti* (liquor manufacturing plants) owners in the form of one-third amount of the liquor sold. A detailed description of the gaddi network and its over all impact on the life of the Hill Korwa has been given elsewhere.[1]

Raw tobacco (*makhur*) is chewed by the Korwa mixing it with lime (*khaini*) mainly by the menfolk. Women and children smoke hand-made cigarettes (*biri*) by rolling dry tobacco powder in the leaf of *sarai* (Shorea-robusta). *Hookah* (hubble-bubble) is used by a few Hill Korwa who are economically and politically dominant. Smoking of *hookah* is considered as a sign of prestige. Common Hill Korwa, however, are not used to it.

It becomes evident that the people still depend on forest and its resources heavily. The nostalgia for *bewar* (shifting cultivation) still lingers with the people and they have not yet developed a technology required for settled agriculture. As a result, they produce only meagre amount of food grains which hardly last for four months in a year. During remaining months of the year they resort to wage labour, hunting and food gathering.

Life Cycle

A Hill Korwa is introduced to various phases of life through a series of characteristic rituals. "The patterns of behaviour as also the social relationship between kins are expressed on these occasions to bring about some order in the social system".[2] Such occasions are important because they authenticate the recognition of an individual with his society on one hand and various degrees of affiliation with his kinsfolk, co-villagers and the neighbours on the other.

The Hill Korwa have some knowledge of the physiological processes involved in child birth. Still they believe that one cannot have a child without the favour of God.

No preference is shown for a male or female child. Sons are welcome as they are helpful in supplementing the family income. "The boy lives permanently in the house while a girl leaves for her husband's house", said Nadi of Rakaiya without necessarily indicating any preference. Budhwa of Rakaiya equally preferred boys and girls. His son Ram Jinis has recently married and wanted a girl as his first issue. He says, "I will keep my daughter in my house and get a husband (ghar-javan) for her. I can ask her for a glass of water and am always sure to get it".

It the advanced stage of pregnancy the expectant mother shifts to an improvised leaf hut (*koamba*) with her husband. The fear of pollution renders her disqualified to participate in ordinary household chores. Touching of the hearth (*chulha*) is a taboo for her. She cannot fetch water, go to forest for collection of fuel and tubers and she is forbidden to carry heavy loads on her head or go near a shrine. A Korwa woman during her pregnancy is debarred from entering into the house through the main door. Hence a small window is made on the back wall (*khirki*) for her exclusive use. While not in use, it is covered with leaves.

An old and experienced woman from amongst the kin helps the parturient mother in delivery. Now, some Korwa families engage services of a Chamatin (woman from the Chamar caste) or Ghasnin (woman of the Ghasia caste) to help during parturition. The umbilical cord and placenta are put into an earthen pitcher and buried in the ground where birth has taken place. The parturient mother is served with rice cooked in turmeric for three days. The child is given a quick bath in hot water immediately after delivery and then is covered in a cotton sheet.

Celebrations associated with birth start on the sixth day after delivery with the hair-cutting ceremony, known as *Chatti*.

It is performed by shaving the child's head hair by an arrow head. Hair cutting is done by the child's father. In case of a male child a tuft of hair is left unshaven just above the occiput. The economically well off Korwa engage the services of barber (Thakur) for hair cutting who is paid Rs. 2/-for the job. The washerman (Dhobi) washes clothes of the parturient mother and receives the same amount. The barber and the washerman are also supplied with uncooked food like some rice, lentils, spices, a chicken and a small quantity of oil.

After hair cutting the child is brought to the open by his father or father's father for showing him to the villagers and members of the clan who make offering in the form of clothes and chicken to the infant's mother.

A nursing woman leaves the *koomba* after 12 days of delivery and having a bath enters into her husband's house.

A name is given to the child by his father or other relatives. There is no fixed time for name giving. During collection of census data it was found that several children in the age group of six months or below had no names. Names are selected on the basis of place and date of birth, time of birth seasonal cycle, trees and economic status of infant's parents, etc.

Table 2.2
Etymology of Common Korwa Names

Names	Sex		Name of days
	Male (M)	Female (Fe)	
Soma	M	—	Som (Monday)
Sumari/Sumri	—	Fe	-do-
Mangra	M	—	Mangal (Tuesday)
Mangni/Mangri	—	Fe	-do-
Budhoo/Budhwa	M	—	Budh (Wednesday)
Budhni	—	Fe	-do-
Biphna	M	—	Biphe (Thursday)
Biphni	—	Fe	-do-
Sukkhoo/Sukkhi/Sukhia	M	—	Sukh (Friday)
Sukhni	—	Fe	-do-
Sanya	M	—	Saniture (Saturday)
Etwa	M	—	Etwar (Sunday)

The above table shows the etymology of selected Korwa names based on seven days of the week. Children born on Monday are given the name Soma or Sumri which is derived from Somwar, the local name of the day. Similarly children born on Tuesday (Mangal) get the names Mangra/Mangri. The suffixes of 'ni' and 'ri' indicate fair sex of the child.

Girls born during the flowering of Mahua get the name Mahuari. Likewise, girls, born in the morning are named Bhinsari and in the evening are Sanjho. Personal qualities, real or fictitious also figure in Korwa names, e.g. Konda (dumb) 'Kondi (female dumb)' Bahra (deaf), Behari (female deaf), Andhoo (blind), Andhi/Andhri (female blind). Name sugges-ting economic status are : Bhikari (the begger), Dukkhi (the woe-be-gotten), Garib (the poor). Girls are also named after birds like Pandki (dove) and Koeli (Quail). Names of months also occur as Korwa names. The following table shows various months of the year figuring in Korwa names.

Table 2.3
Korwa Names After Months

Names	Male (M)	Female (Fe)	Months	English Equivalent
Chatoo/Saitoa	M	—	Chait	March-April
Baisakhoo	M	—	Baisakh	April-May
Baisakhi	M	Fe	-do-	-do-
Jethoo	M	—	Jeth	May-June
Asroo	M	—	Asadh	June-July
Asri	—	Fe	-do-	-do-
Launa	M	—	Sawan	July-August
Sauni	—	Fe	-do-	-do-
Bhado	M	—	Bhado	August-September
Kuwri	—	Fe	Kuwar	September-October
Katika	M	—	Kartik	October-November
Aghnoo	M	—	Aghan	November-December
Aghni	—	Fe	-do-	-do-
Poosa	M	—	Poos	December-January
Magoo	M	—	Magh	January-February
Maghni	—	Fe	-do-	-do-
Phagoo	M	—	Phagum	Febuary-March
Phagni	—	Fe	-do-	-do-

Breast feeding of a child continues till the birth on the next issue. Children are given solid food from the age of six months. A one year old child eats millet-cakes, boiled roots, beans, mahua flowers, and drinks handi (home made bear).

Initiation

Children come to know about the mysteries of sex from an early age of six or seven years. This is the time when they start grazing cattle in forests.Sexual behaviour of animals make an impact on their minds and they also imitate sexual play amongst themselves. Small Korwa dwelling units help further crystallising their ideas about sex. Sexual acts by youngsters provokes jesting among the elders. With the coming of age and sexual intimacy, Korwa parents come to know about the choice of their children. At the age of 13 to 14 years in case of boys and 10 to 11 years in case of girls formal engagement (*mangabara*) is performed. This removes all barriers against sexual intimacy of the two loving hearts. No restriction is imposed on sex after *mangabara* and the couple enjoy full freedom to procreate. The mode of enticing a girl is to offer her a packet of birds, a bottle of liquor, a few ornaments, and if one can afford a piece of sari. Lovers meet in the forest and during *dumkach* dances. The two slip away for a short while for love making in an isolated place. A vigorous dancer, full of life and vitality, is called *rasia* and he receives favours from many young beauties. Similarly, an astute dancer possessing a healthy body, *rupni*, is heavily chased after by young boys in order to win her favour.

Satisfaction of sex is the main theme of Korwa love making . If a boy is unable to satisfy a mature girl or if a girl is too young to give an active co-operation to a mature boy in sexual contacts they separate without any hesitation and choose other partners.

Pre-marital sex relations are confined within the tribes between members of different clans. Breach of this rule is a punishable offence. The traditional Korwa Panchyat yet is responsible for regulation of sexual behaviour of the members of the tribe. Sexual involvement with a girl belonging to another tribe is an offence of severe order that results in ostracization of the erring individual.

About a couple of years ago Poosa of Rouni village (District Raigarh) eloped with an Oraon girl and settled in a village in Surguja. The two were hotly chased, caught, and brought back to their respective villages. This affair caused a serious tension between the Oraon and the Korwa and the relatives of the Oraon girl threatened to kill the Korwa boy. The elders (*sayana*) of Sardapath village sent a deputation to the Oraon for settlement. This deputation consisted of the Korwa Patel, a Korwa Panch (member of statutory Panchayat) and the Kotwar of the village. They pleaded guilty before the Oraon and begged apologies by promising to punish the culprit. Later, the Korwa Panchayat was called at Sardapath in which the Oraon *sayana* were also invited. The Oraon demanded a fine of Rs.500/- from the Hill Korwa but after much bargaining they came down to Rs.140/-. The money was paid in cash by the father of the offender. The Korwa gave an undertaking to the Oraon that in the event of recurrence of similar offence of the former will pay Rs.1,000/- to the latter. The members of the guilty household were excommunicated by the Panchayat till the family gave a punitive feast (*panch-patri*) seeking reunion with the tribe.

Sexual relation within the clan is highly discouraged and the society grants recognition to such unions only after the punitive feast. If defaulters escape to some other far off village, they cease to exist for their kin unless they return to their respective villages and face the traditional panchayat, pay up the penalty imposed on them by the council of elders (Panchayat) and reunite with the tribe.

Cases of intra-clan sexual relations were neither reported from the Rakaiyanor from Bansajhal. Out of 204 marital alliances only one case was reported from Maltipur and five other cases from Sardapath.

Negotiations for Biah

Marriage (*biah*) is not only essential for gratification of sexual desires but it helps the people to maintain the continuity of group and regulate labour supply. Remaining single for a Korwa is unthinkable unless he or she suffers from some physical handicap.

Age at marriage of a Korwa boy or girl cannot be categorically specified as it is closely linked with economic status of the families concerned. Relatively well off Korwa families prefer to marry their children at an early age.

Libra, the Patel of Jampani (Surguja) got his daughter Sukhni married at her eight years of age with a boy of 10 years. He had a good harvest that year and as he did not know about the prospects in future he chose that time.

Poor families postpone children's marriages till they get a good crop and stock enough grain to brew as much as 20 pitchers of *handi* (beer).

Sahdeo of Sardapath was working as farm labourer in the fields of Harya Ram in order to save some money for his marriage of his father Tahloo expressed his inability io bear the expenditure toward his son's marriage.

Physically handicapped of either sex mostly remain unmarried. Sauna of Rakaiya (65 years old) remained unmarried due to blindness and was living with his elder brother's son. Epiliptic Jarha of Laldara had the same fate. Konda (dumb) of Patratoli and Kondi (female dumb) of Rakaiya were rather fortunate to find suitable match in each other and married at the age of 33 and 28 respectively. A boy is normally married at the age of 15 years and a girl 13 to 14 years.

It has already been said earlier that the sexual life of a Korwa boy and girl starts early. The intimacy of a boy and a girl is never looked down upon by the society. Parents keep a watchful eye on their children and come to know about their children towards their respective consorts. If living in the same village the lovers pass sufficient time with each other but if they happen to live in separate villages, they meet in the adjoining forests, weekly markets, in fairs and festivals and make a decision. Formal negotiations are initiated by a mediator (*agua*). The *agua* negotiates with the bride's parents on behalf of the groom's parents. If his proposal gets a favourable response from bride's side the elders of the two concerned families meet on a place fixed by the *agua* in order to fix the amount of bride price.

The prospective groom's party is received by the bride's parents and elders of her village. The bride's (*kanya*) father entertains the guests with liquor. After fixation of the bride-price (*sukhsarha*) the two parties fix a date for *mangabara* in consultation with the *Baigas* of respective villages. When the negotiations ripen, the bride groom's (*bar*) father offers a pair of clothes consisting of a blouse (*jhoola*) and a sari (*sohane*) and a red bead necklace (*guria*) to the bride. From this day *dumkach* dance is performed daily in the evening till the *mangabara*.

The amount of bride-piice depends on the prrsonal merits of the bride and the economic status of her family. The minimum amount of bride-price was found Rs. 14/-and the maximum was Rs.125. The Hill Korwa blame the neighbouring tribes for a spurt in the bride-price. High prices of consumer goods was stated to be another factor responsible for it. The amount of bride-price is paid at the time of *biah* but the responsibility of the bride's maintenance falls on the bridegroom's father from the day of negotiated settlement.

Mahru of Rakaiya settled his son's marriage with Nadi's daughter. In the first year after settlement of negotiation, he presented clothes to the bride worth Rs.1/- in the second year worth Rs.2/- and in the third year worth Rs.3.

The amount of bride-price is distributed among various kin of the bride. Mother, being the begetter of her daughter, is entitled to a lion's share. The remaining amount is equally divided among her relatives.

Mangabara literally means "acquiring the groom" for a girl. Unlike *biah* in which turmeric is applied on bodies of the couple, in *mangabara* only oil is anointed.

Mangabara Ceremony

On the day of *mangabara*, the bridegroom comes in a procession to the bride's place. As soon as the groom's party arrives, sisters and collaterals wash feet of all guests with warm water. The bridegroom's father brings six pitchers of home made beer (*handi*) and a chicken, which are offered to the spirits of bride's ancestors. He also brings a pair of clothes, bead necklaces and bangles for the bride. The bride's father entertains the guests with country beer, which is generally followed by a feast. This is, however, not obligatory on the part of bride's father to offer food.

The bride's and bridegroom's party sits separately facing each other. The bride's father's brother's wife or father's sister in the absence of the former carries the bride in the open in her lap and makes the latter sit in front of the hut. Similarly the bridegroom is brought out and made to sit beside the bride either by the father's brother's wife or the father's sister. The bride is wrapped in a single piece of cloth dyed yellow in turmeric. The groom also wears the same dress.

No sooner the couple comes out and sits together, the two Kotwars of the two villages stand in front of each other and exchange the following dialogue.

Groom's Kotwar : Kutumb Maharaj, hamaar ek baat sunal jai. Apan bigral dharti ma ham Konhra ka ek beej dara wah beej phurnai gael. Okar ek larank purab gava, ek larank pachim gava, ek dakhin gava, ek uttar gava. Uttar panjon; dakhin panjon; pachim. panjon Panjat panjat okar ek larank purab gava. Wahi larank ka phoal haman lewai awa haun.

English rendering of above dialogue

Listen to us respected affines. In my barren land, I sowed a seed of pumpkin, the seed germinated and became a creeper. One of its branches reached towards west, another to south, the third one to north and last one to the east. I searched its branches in the west, south and north. One of its branches came in the east (direction of the bride's village) and I have come to get the flower from the same branch.

Bride's Kotwar : Phool lebe ki phar ? (you want flower or fruit ?)

Groom's Kotwar : Phool lehun (I want flower).

Bride's Kotwar : Hamaar phool kana hai (My flower is rotten and deformed).

Groom's Kotwar : Hamaar phar be kana hai; ham kanha phool leb. Kanha hoi to oka seejhai leb. (My fruit is also rotten and deformed. Hence, I will take rotten and deformed flower. If it is so, we will make it alright).

Bride's Kotwar : Mor tor, tor mor, toot phoot, nisi-disi ma sau rupya ki jaban (Mine is yours and yours is mine). In case of break (of engagement) or bad conduct, I promise to pay you one hundred rupees.

Groom's Kotwar : Sau rupya ki jaban (I also promise to pay you one hundred rupees).

The above dialogues are known as *sawal-jawab*. As soon as the agreement is reached, the two Kotwars and members of the respective parties embrace each other. Young boys and girls of the bride's village perform *dumakach* dance. Boys insist hesitant sisters of the groom to join them in the dance spree which is performed in the accompaniment of *mander* (two sided drums) and *dapla* (one sided drum). In the mean-time the Kotwar ties the end of the cloth of the bride with that of the bridegroom. The couple moves round the crowd with folded hands and utters 'Ram-Ram', bowing their heads a little. This is called *johar*. In return of *johar* the couple receives blessings and gifts from the crowd.

After *johar*, the bride leaves her relatives and joins the in-laws. Pleasantries are exchanged between the affines with periodic distribution of raw tobacco among male folk. The assembly disperses in the afternoon. The bride also leaves along with her husband. After this ceremony the couple live as husband and wife. In fact the trial of married life begins only after completion of the *mangabara*. If either of the two spouses is not satisfied he or she can desert the other. In case of a girl deserting the boy after *mangabara*, her parents pay back the expenses incurred in *mangabara* to the opposite party.

Biah is a modified version of *mangabara* in which turmeric is massaged on the bodies of husband and wife. Sometimes *mangabara* and biah ceremonies are performed simultaneously if the parents of the two spouses agree for the same. Otherwise *mangabara* precedes *biah*. Leaving the turmeric massage ceremony (hardi charhana) aside, the ceremonies of mangabara and biah are similar. If a person does not perform *biah* ceremony after his *mangabara*, he is considered defiled. He is supposed to become a ghost (*masan*) after his death. Similarly a girl becomes a witch (ohuri) if she does not undergo the turmeric massage ceremony.

There is a belief that a Korwa will reborn as a Korwa in his or her respective clan. A ghost is not entitled to ancestor worship. Hence, *biah* is considered essential even after birth of two or three children in order to maintain the continuity further of rebirths. However, those who do not perform *biah* do not face any social sanction during their present life but they face the consequences of their ommission after their death. The Korwa society, therefore, looks down upon those who do not undergo *biah* ceremonies.

The intervening period between *mangabara* and *biah* is not fixed. The observance of the latter depends on the economic condition and mutual convenience of the two respective families. A landless and poor boy belonging to a landless family is supposed to meet his marriage expenses by resorting to labour.

Konda of Patratoli, Surguja, a dumb boy of 33 years worked as a labourer with a prominent Kawar of the area for five years. He saved enough money to marry a girl of Rakaiya who was also a dumb, but unfortunately could not get money from his employer. Hence, the marriage expenses of the boy were entirely borne by the girl's father.

Sahdeo of Sardapath (Raigarh) was engaged but his *biah* was delayed because of the fact that at the time of his elder brother's marriage his father had spent all his savings and expressed his inability to meet the marriage expenses of his next son. So, Sahdeo was working as a labourer in the fields of Harya Ram in order to procure money for his *biah*.

Biah Ceremonies

Biah is not treated as confirmed unless the amount of bride-price is paid to the bride's father and the couple goes under *hardicharai* (turmeric massage) ceremony.

The date of marriage is fixed by the Baiga. Seven days before the marriage millets are put to boil and kept for brewing. The village boys and girls perform *dumkach* dance at the residence of both the bride (*kanya*) and bridegroom (*bar*) every day till marriage is over. On the day of marriage the near kin and prominent villagers are invited by the boy's father and are served with refreshment (naasta) before they proceed to the bride's residence.

As soon as the wedding procession (*baraat*) reaches at bride's residence, the feet of all members of bridal procession are washed with warm water. This is the usual Korwa style for welcoming guests as they believe that guests come to them after walking a long distance. Hence, their feet should be given immediate relief. After washing of feet the guests are led towards *madua,* a place which is specially built for the performance of marriage ceremonies. It is in the shape of a raised platform of about ten square feet plastered with mud and cow-dung and thatched with green shrubs. The members of wedding procession sit near the *madua* and are served with handi in leaf cups soon after their arrival.

The marriage ceremonies start with *mitti-korai* (digging of soil) by the Baiga of the village. Five green wooden poles are kept in conical shape at the place where the Baiga digs the soil by a shovel. The bride's father's brother's wife sits behind the Baiga spreading an end of her sari. The Baiga digs the soil and throws it towards the woman sitting behind without looking at her. The woman collects the soil and takes it to the *madua.* The soil dug by the Baiga is kept in the centre of the *madua.* The Baiga demands a dhoti or Rs 2/- in lieu of his services. The payment is made in cash or promised by the bride's father to be paid in future. The bride's father is supported by his relatives if he pleads his incapability to make payment in cash immediately. The Baiga agrees to accept the payment at a later date. Ronha of Rakaiya, during his daughter's marriage narrated his difficulties to the Baiga in following words : "I am a poor man. I had a bad harvest and am deeply indebted and unable to keep my daughter with me. Hence I am giving her to a stranger. Her husband will look after her and provide her meals. How can I give you money ?" The Baiga accepted bride's father's plea and deferred his demand for future. He, however, demanded *handi* which was readily provided.

After completion of *mitti-korai* ceremony, the poles are dismantled. One pole is fixed in the centre of the *madua* and four poles are fixed in four corners of it. Agreement (*sawal-jawab*) is reached between the two parties. The wordings of the agreement are similar to those uttered during the *manga-bara* ceremony which have already been described.

After reaching the contract, members of the two party embrace one another. The *bar* offers handi to the *kanya* and the latter reciprocates. It is a symbolical pledge taken by the *bar* that as a husband he will offer meals first to his wife and accept without any fuss whatever she offers to him. Now, the *bar* offers liquor to the earth. It is an offering made to the deceased ancestors imploring a prosperous and happy married life. The *kanya* reciprocates the act. After making an offering to the earth the Baiga offers *handi* to the respective mothers of the couple.

After completion of the above mentioned ceremonies the stage becomes set for turmeric massage. This is performed in two parts :

Hardi-charchnna (upward turmeric massage) and *Hardi-utarana* (downward turmeric massage). The former ceremony is the testimony of the fact that the *kanya* is a virgin while the latter ceremony is a symbolic declaration that she is no more a virgin and belongs to the *bar*.

Bar's brothers' wives,sisters, and female cousin massage turmeric on the body of the *kanya* and the similar relatives of the *kanya* reciprocate the ceremony for the *bar*. Elderly ladies do not usually participate in this ceremony.

The upward turmeric massage starts from feet, covers the entire body and completes with forehead. After completion of the each round of massage, the *bàr* and *kanya* clinging on the back of a girl participate in *bhanwari* dance around the central pole of *madua*. *Bar's* sisters hold the bride in turns and the *bar* is held by the bride's sisters. This ceremony lasts for the whole night and each round of massage is followed by *bhanwari* and *dumkach* dances. The ceremony comes to an end at dawn with the breakfast consisting of rice covered with a thin layer of lentil-broth served in leafy cups.

After a pause of two hours, the *bar* and *kanya* are given a bath. The water for bathing is fetched by the sisters and female cousins of the bride. Each of them gets quarter of a rupee from the bride's father. Mothers of the couple stretch the front end of their saris like a canopy over the couple's heads. The Kotwar of bride's village then tosses a pitcher filled with water with full force above the heads of the couple. The Kotwar of groom's village hits the pitcher with an axe when in air, breaking it into pieces. The water falls on heads of the couple. The ceremony is known as *pani katna* or cutting water. After *pani-katna* ceremony the couple is given a full bath, clothes are changed, and they are brought under the *madua* once again. In the meantime the affines indulge in joking, throwing mud water on one another.

The bridegroom then pours mustard oil on the hairparting of the bride's head through a mango leaf. The oil streaks down towards the forehead. If the oil goes straight and does not spill out of the hair-parting, the bride is believed to be very lucky. The remaining oil is given to married women who apply it on their heads.

Now, the couple come out from *madua* and sit on a small mound of paddy cushioned by palm leaves for receiving gifts from the crowd. This ritual is known as *chumban*, the young boys of the two side implore the crrowd to make presentations to the couple uttering "*bārso, barso aage barso.pecho barso*" (rain, rain, rain in the front and rain behind). Parents of the bridegroom are the first to present the bride a few ornaments made of aluminium, a piece of cloth and a few coins worth about a rupee. Then comes the turn of other relations to make presents. All of a sudden the joyous atmosphere takes a tuin toward melancholy. The mother of the bride cries bitterly so also her brothers and sisters and other women of the village irrespective of their kinship affiliation. The old ladies however, try to console the bride's mother and her younger siblings telling them that the bride is going to a new house where she will find a new set of parents (in-laws), grand parents, uncles, and aunts and will get their affection if she remains faithful and obedient to her husband. She must not murmur even if injustice is incurred on her. She should feel happy that she is going to such a good house and must not cry.

After completion of the *chumban* ceremony the loose ends of the couple's robes are tied together to a knot and the couple pay *johar* to all those present in the gathering and receive blessings from them.

Marriage expenses are mainly borne by the bride-groom's father. The bride's father however, promises to present her daughter a cow or a calf as *dahaj* (dowry) but it is not considered essential. The bridegroom's father accepts the responsibility providing *hadia* and a feast not only to his agnates but also to affines.

A modest Korwa marriage costs between Rs. 200/-and Rs. 300/-in addition to the bride-price. Saitoo of Bankheta (Surguja) paid a bride-price of Rs. 120/- and arranged the following articles :

Mustard Oil	— 1 litre
Millets	— 7 maunds for (2. 8 quintals) for brewing 12 pitchers of handi
Rice	— 6 maunds for feast
Pulses	— 1 maund
Salt	— 3 kgs
Ronou/jari	— Rs.11/-for brewing handi

Pig/Goat	— 1 (Rs. 40/-)
Turmeric	— 2 kgs
Sari for kanya	— 1 (Rs.4/-)
Dhoti for kanya's elder brother	— 1 (Rs.2/-)

Gharjawain Marriage

In *gharjawai* marriage, the bridegroom stays with his bride's parents and does not pay any bride-price. The marriage is negotiated through services of *Agua* in the manner which has already been described. *Gharjawain* marriage involves the bridegroom in a five year's contract with his parents-in-law on the following conditions :

1. The bridegroom will have to live with his parents-in-law for a minimum period of five years and should serve them in any manner they deem fit.

2. He will not inherit any right over bride's father's land. The latter may, however, gift a portion of land to the former from his share of land.

3. The bridegroom's parents will be exempted from paying the bride-price.

4. If the the bridegroom wants to leave his wife before the expiry of the stipulated period, he will have to refund the expenses incurred on his maintenance. But if divorce or desertion takes place from the bride's side, her father will have to return the expenses to the bridegroom's father which he has incurred in marriage.

The ceremonies involved in *gharjawain* marriages are similar to those performed in *biah* already described.

The two following cases from Rakaiya will narrate :

Gharjawain Marriages

1. Manager's father (of Patratoli village) died when the former was young. After his father's death Manager lived with his *pitya-kaka* (father's younger brother) as his mother remarried Bajroo of Rakaiya. Bajroo refused to accept Manager because he already had two daughters from his

deceased previous wife. Manager became the *gharjawain* of Sukkhan of the same village at the age often years. After three years' stay, Sukkhan married his daughter Chuli to Manager. Now Manager is working as an agricultural labourer on a salary of Rs. 22/- per month and gives his earnings to his wife. In his spare time he works in Sukkhan's fields. He is living in a part of Sukkhan's house but is thinking of building his own house soon after the birth of his first issue.

2. Ronha of Rakaiya got his deaf and dumb daughter married with a deaf and dumb boy Patratoli named Konda and brought him at his house as *gharjawain.* As an old man of 75 years of age, Ronha had no male issue to look after him. His second wife came with two daughters of her former husband. Ronha's three sons from earlier wife Sukkhan, Budhwa and Mangra were married and living separately in their respective houses. Ronha divided his lands equally among them and kept a portion of land for himself. Having no other male issue he thought it expedient to bring a *gharjawain.* He was so eager that he accepted to bear all the expenses of his daughter's marriage which is contrary to the accepted Korwa norm in which it is the bridegroom's father's responsibility to meet the expenses of marriage. Ronha's three son's got anoyed to see their father's over enthusiasm in the marriage and refused to share the expenses of their half sister's marriage. Ronha's sons were angry because they visualised the possibility of Ronaha's land being transferred to Konda by the former's will instead of coming to them after Ronahas death. Secretly, they also decided to drive Konda out of the village soon after the marriage so that the land may not go to the stranger.

Sagai Marriage

Sagai marriages are those in which a person re-marries after the death or desertion of either of the two spouses. The difference between *biah* and *sagai* is that the latter is less elaborate than the former. In case when both the spouses remarry only oil massage is given instead of the turmeric massage. If either of the two is unmarried he/she will be given turmeric massage. Another difference is of timing. *Biah* usually takes place during night and food is served for a minimum of two times but *sagai* is performed during day time and usually in the afternoon. The Hill Korwa assume that people usually come to attend *sagai* after having meals at their respective homes and thus no meals need to be served to the guests. It was noticed that in *sagai* only *handi* is served. It was, however, reported that in the past when the Hill Korwa were more prosperous, *sagai* was to be performed with as much elan as in *biah*.

The amount of bride-price is less in the case of *sagai*. Koka of Rakaiya paid Rs. 40/- to the parents of his wife but after his widow remarried Sukkhoo, who paid only Rs. 12/- to her parents as the amount of bride-price.

The group of spouses in *sagai* seemed higher than what it is in *biah* but in some cases it was found that young bachelors married widows by paying a lower amount of bride-price. Such persons belonged to the impoverished section of the society. Rituals and festivities involved in *sagai* marriages are similar to those of *biah*.

In the preceding pages, only those methods of Korwa marriages have been described which are prescribed and sanctioned by the Korwa society. But deviations from the laid-down conventions, norms, and laws of marriage by the society are accepted by the Korwa as likely occurrences and the Korwa society has the mechanism of normalising them.

Urharia

Marriage resulting frcm extra-marital relations of two previously married persons is known as *urharia*. When any such clandestine sexual liaison comes on the surface either of the two aggrieved parties brings the matter before the *jat-panchayat*, a body consisting of village elders (*sayana*) who try to find out the initial offender. If the man is found at fault, he is asked by the panchayat to pay the bride-price at an enhanced rate to the husband of the woman involved in *urharia*. If the woman is found at fault, she is deserted by her husband. So long she remains unmarried after the desertion she or her parents need not pay back the amount of bride-price but no sooner she remarries, her new husband is asked by the *panchayat* to pay the amount of bride-price back to her former husband. In such cases, the amount of bride-price remains unchanged.

Dhuku

The other mode of acquiring mates against the prescribed norms of the society is *dhuku,* according to which a bachelor or married brings an unmarried girl of his choice against the wishes of his and her parents. If a girl develops a soft-corner for the boy, she goes to live with him against the wishes of her suitor's parents who make every effort to drive her out of their home. But if she remains steadfast in her determination not to leave the house of her lover inspite of all indignities and humiliation meted out to her by her in-laws, she is permitted to stay and the amount of bride-price demanded by the girl's parents is paid and the marriage is regularised. If a married person performs *dhuku* with a maiden, he pays the bride-price fixed by the panchayat consisting of two members of the two respective clans and the elders of the village. Parents of the two involved families also participate in the deliberations of the *panchayat*.

If the *panchayat* fails to arrive at a decision, the matter is referred to the Lotadar for his decision. Even if the Lotadar fails to decide the matter, it is settled by a showdown of force.

The following case study for Patratoli will help to explain the nature and process of *urharia* marriages :

Singra, an old man of about 75 years remarried. His wife came to him with her deceased daughter's daughter who was an unmarried teenager. The old man developed intimacy with the young girl which resulted into the latter's pregnancy. The girl confessed that she was carrying Singra's child. This infuriated the girl's paternal kin living in Rakaiya who demanded Singra's ex-communication and held him guilty of indulging in sex with an orphan and a member of alternate descending generation. As the girl had lost both her parents and her only guardian was the wife of the offender, the amount of bride-price was fixed considerably low. Singra paid Rs.16/- as the amount of bride-price to Budhwa of Rakaiya and Rs.20/- for liquor to be consumed by the *sayanas*, who participated in the *panchayat* deleberations. Singra's two sons Etwa, 50 years and Mahra, 45 years gave an undertaking to the girl's paternal kin that they will take the responsibility for the maintenance of their young mother and the child to be born to her in event of their father's death. The *panchayat* permitted Singra to marry the girl after giving the penalty feast (*panch-patri*). He was also asked to arrange the marriage before the baby is born. Pending the punitive feast Singra was ex-communicated. After a lapse of four months, Singra remarried with the girl and the girl had to undergo turmeric massage (*hardi-charhai*) ceremoney as she was a virgin. The following diagram elucidates the case mentioned above :

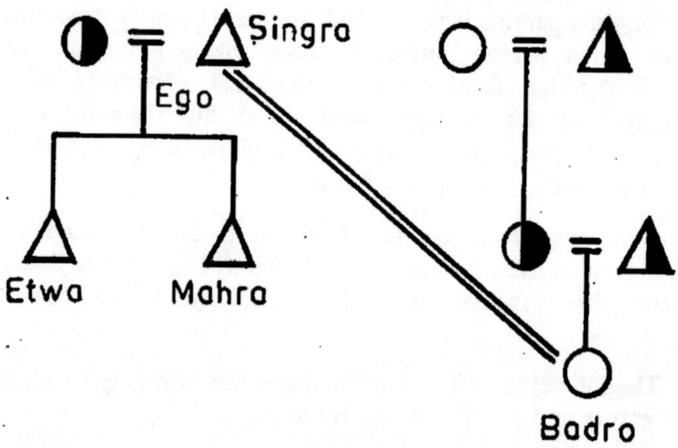

Diagram 2.2

The Table 2.4 depicts various methods of acquiring mates.

Biah is the most popular method. The study of 204 marital alliances shows 128 cases of *biah*. In Bansajhal out of 49 couples, 37 acquired their mates through *biah* (75.51 per cent). Bansajhal is closely followed by Maltipur in this respect where out of 42 married couples 31 had acquired their mates through *biah* (73.81 per cent). Sardapath, and Rakaiya show a similar rating. In Sardapath, out of 77 married couples 41 have acquired mates through *biah* (53.25 per cent) and in Rakaiya out of 36, 19 couples performed *biah* (52.78 per cent).

Sagai comes next to *biah* through which 32 couples out of 204 couples (15.69 per cent) have acquired their mates. Rakaiya shows the maximum number of *sagai*. The table shows that out of 36 married couples in Rakaiya 10 couples (27.78 per cent) have performed *sagai*. Bansajhal comes next where out of 49 couples, eight have acquired their mates through *sagai* (16.32 per cent). Out of 42 married couples in Maltipur, six have performed *sagai* (14.29 per cent). Sardapath comes last in this respect where out of 77 married couples only 8 have performed *sagai* (10.39 percent). The above data suggest that the frequency of *sagai* marriages can be linked with the economy of the respective village. A village in economic hardships like Rakaiya shows the maximum number of *sagai* marriages whereas relatively prosperous Hill Korwa of Sardapath show a lower frequency of *sagai*.

Acquiring a mate through *gharjawain* (uxorilocal) marriage is not a popular one. Only 11 cases of *gharjawain* were recorded out of the total number of 204 marital alliances. Rakaiya, Maltipur and Bansajhal show one case each and Sardapath shows 8 cases.

Factors responsible for a low frequency of *gharjawain* are as below :

a. Poor economy

Gharjawain marriages are performed by relatively richer Korwa families. The three villages studied in Surguja show uniform figure of one *gharjawain* each as these villages may be put more or less at a similar plane of economic prosperity while Sardapath, where the Hill Korwa are relatively better off, there are 8 cases of *gharjawain* marriages (10.39 percent).

TABLE 2.4

Methods of Acquiring Mates

Methods	Rakaiya	Percent-age	Maltipur	Percent-age	Bansajhal	Percent-age	Sardapath	Percent-age	Total	Percent-age
Biah	19	52.78	31	73.81	37	75.51	41	53.25	128	62.75
Sagai	10	27.78	6	14.29	8	16.32	8	10.39	32	15.69
Gharjawain	1	2.78	1	2.38	1	2.04	8	10.39	11	5.39
Mangabara	4	11.10	2	4.76	2	2.08	2	2.60	10	4.90
Udarhia	2	5.56	2	4.76	—	–	2	2.60	6	2.94
Dhuku	—	–	—	–	1	2.04	16	20.77	17	8.33
Total	36	100.00	42	100.00	49	100.00	77	100.00	204	100.00

b. Social prestige

As stated earlier, only better off Korwa families can think of bringing a *gharjawain*. Persons selected as *gharjawain* mostly belong to poorer and landless Korwa families and sometime are treated rather shabbily by their affines. The status of a *gharjawain* is considered lower than one who has acquired his wife through *biah*. By virtue of his dependency over his father-in-law and wife, the status of a *gharjawain* is a combination of a servant and a kin, until he establishes his new household and starts earning to run his household independently.

Mangabara

Ten cases of *mangabara* came to notice out of 204 marital alliances. Rakaiya reported 4 cases, whereas Maltipur, Bansajhal and Sardapath reported 2 cases each. It was told in the beginning that people report to mangabara and produce children because of economic stringencies. No sooner they acquire sufficient resources, they convert *mangabara* into *biah*. The main cause behind relatively higher incidence of *mangabara* in Rakaiya is their overall poverty.

Deviations from the approved norms of marriage are visible in Korwa society like any other human society. *Biah sagai*, *gharjawain* and *mangabara* are the approved forms of acquiring mates. There are certain other modes of acquiring mates which are not approved by the society and set the mechanism of marriage regulation in motion. The system is operated and controlled by the traditional *jat panchayat*, particularly in cases of *urharia* and *dhuku*. Study of 204 marital alliances shows cases of deviation from the accepted rules, norms, and conventions of marriage. The number of deviant cases are 23 (11.27 per cent.)

The frequency of *dhuku* was found to be 8.33 per cent among the Hill Korwa, 2.04 per cent in Bansajhal and 20.77 per cent in Sardapath. No cases were found at Rakaiya and Maltipur.

The high frequency of *dhuku* marriage at Sardapath may be attributed to the following factors :

a. Capability to pay back the bride-price appears higher in Sardapath than in other villages. While discussing *ghar-jawain* marriages earlier it was said that the Hill Korwa of Sardapath are relatively more prosperous than their brethren in the remaining three villages.

b. Another factor conducive to *dhuku* marriages is that a man with considerable landed property is considered favourite among the Korwa women. The data show that all those who performed *dhuku* marriages possessed relatively bigger landholdings.

c. The Hill Korwa Sardapath asserted that the tendency of higher occurrence of *dhuku* marriages is a direct result of their contact with neighbouring castes like the Mahtos (Ahir) and tribes viz. Oraon, Nagesia.

Monogamy

It was found that the majority of the Korwa marital unions, i.e., 85.79 per cent, are monogamous. If levirate and sororate marriages are also taken into account, the proportion of monogamy rises to 88.73 per cent. Rakaiya is characterised by the highest number of monogamous marriages (94.44 per cent). Sardapath comes next with 90.91 per cent monogamous marriages. Maltipur had relatively lower proportion of monogamy (85.79 per cent) and Bansajhal occupies the lowest place in this respect with 75.51 per cent monogamous unions.

Polygyny

No cases of polygyny came to notice at Rakaiya. Maltipur showed 5 cases of pologyny, Bansajhal and Sardapath had 6 cases each. The overall frequency of polygyny among the people is 8.33 per cent. It was further observed that out of 23 cases of polygyny eight were performed due to barrenness of the first wife. Most of the people who married subsequently were holding some important posts in the traditional *jat panchayat* or statutory panchayat. In Sardapatha Hill Korwa Primary School Teacher was found having two wives.

Sororal Polygyny

Out of 23 cases of polygyny, six were of sororal polygyny. According to custom a man can marry the younger sister of his living wife.

Dhansai, the son of Chandra Patel of Maltipur married Kundna and had a son from her. After two years he married the younger sister of Kundna. It may be mentioned that the father of the said man possesses 16 acres of land.

Ronha of Bansajhal married Baisakhi and subsequently he performed *dhuku* with Noli, who was the former wife of his father's elder brother's son. He married for the third time with Noli's younger sister, who was previously married to his own younger brother. Because of the last marriage, Ronha was ex-communicated from the tribe due to breach of the laws of avoidance for marrying his younger brother's wife. Ronha's father Sukhi had 43.14 acres of land.

Baisakhoo, son of Harya Ram, the Panch of Sardapath statutory panchayat married Chanhi, who subsequently brought her younger sister through *dhuku*. Harya Ram owns 24.98 acres of land.

The above cases clearly show that among the Hill Korwa those who practice polygyny generally possess bigger landholdings. The poorer section of the society generally practice monogamy.

Sororate

In case of sororate, when a man marries the younger sister of his deceased wife, no bride-price is paid. The Hill Korwa believe that the amount of bride-price paid for the previous wife remains intact after her death and it is the obligation on the part of the parents of his deceased wife to make available another daughter to the husband of their deceased daughter who has already paid the amount. This is however, not always followed. The attraction of bride-price entices the parents of the deceased woman to marry their younger daughters elsewhere. There were several cases where the deceased woman did not have any younger sister who could be offered to the bereaved man.

Cross-cousion marriage

The Hill Korwa allow marriage with mother's brother's daughter and father's sister's daughter. The frequency of marriage with mother's brother's daughter was found higher than with the father's sister's daughter. The frequency of cross-cousin marrriage is low and only two such cases were recorded from Rakaiya.

Rules of marriage

The Hill Korwa observe the following rules of marriage breach of which amounts to offence.

1. Marriage with member of the same clan or outside the fold of the tribe is strictly prohibited.
2. Marriage with the Dehari Korwa is an offence though not of very serious nature.
3. Marriage with parallel cousin, half-sibling or with a member of alternate generations is also prohibited.
4. Mairiage with relatives with whom the rule of avoidance is observed is prohibited.

Breaches, however, are not absent and were reported from Maltipur, Bansajhal, and Sardapath particularly of the nature of clan exogamy.

TABLE 2.5

Incidences of Clan Endogamy Among The Hill Korwa

Villages	No. of marital alliances	Clan-endogamy	Percentage
Rakaiya	36	—	—
Maltipur	42	1	2.38
Bansajhal	49	2	4.08
Sardapath	77	5	6.49
Total	204	8	12.95

The above table shows that 8 cases of clan endogamy were recorded together from Maltipur, Bansajhal, and Sardapath.

One case of tribal exogamy in which a Hill Korwa woman married a member of the Majhi tribe was recorded from Bansajhal.

One case of inter-marriage with Kodaku came to notice from Jonkapath village, 5 miles north-east of Shankargarh Police Station (District Surguja).

One case from Laldhara, a village situated in Jonkapath Hills, was reported in which a Hill Korwa woman eloped with a Dehari Korwa.

A case of marriage between the members of alternate generation, described earlier in details was recorded from Patratoli, a village near Rakiay.

Regulation of marriage rule

The breach of clan exogamy incurs a penalty of severe nature or financial implication. The offenders are ostracized forthwith from the tribe along with their respective families. Smoking, drinking and dining with the penalised families amounts to an offence. Any person extending the co-operation to the ex-communicated families also loses the right of membership of the society. The penalty imposed by the *jat panchayat* for committing the offence of clan-endogamy is known as *panch-patri.*

Birjhoo, the ex-Lotadar of Biria gave the following list of articles required for a *panch-patri* feast :

Rice	— 12 Maunds	Rs. 672.00
A Pig or Goat	—	Rs. 40.00
Handi	— 20 pitchers	Rs. 110.00
Liquor	— 5 bottles	Rs. 10.00
Pulses	— 3 maunds	Rs. 120.00
Mustard oil	— 3 litres	Rs. 15.00
Spices	—	Rs. 10.00
	Total	Rs. 10.77

The total cost of panch-patri. as shown in the above table is Rs. 977. A *biah,* on the other can be easily performed were

Rs. 300. Thus, the expenses involved in the punitive panch-patri feast show an increase slightly more than three times. The cost of *panch-patri* is staggering and back breaking for an average Korwa family.

The *panch-patri* generally consists of 4 Korwa elders representing Murihar, Hasddwar, Edigwar, and Samadwar clan of the Korwa and a Hindu who is invariably a member of the Mahto caste.

First of all food is served to the five above mentioned people and then to the other participants. The member of caste Hindu included in *panch-patri* does not accept cooked food from the Hill Korwa, instead he is offered un-cooked food grains and oil and spices.

When the feast is over, the Lotadar raises a metallic vessel (lota) filled with liquor and requests the participants to accept the liquor. The Lotadar drinks first from vessel and then it is passed on to each participant in turn. Whosoever receives the lota, dips his index finger in the liquor and puts it on the front of his tongue. This is the symbolic consent of members of the tribe for the re-unification of offenders with the tribe.

Marriage outside the tribe was an unpardonable offence in the past and the ex-communicated couple had to leave the village to start a new life. Now, the offenders seek re-union with the tribe through *panch-patri*.

The Korwa attitude towards marital union is very practical. In order to avoid the payment of bride-price the society has evolved *mangabara* and *gharjawain* methods of marriages. In some cases the payment involved is deferred indefinitely in order to give relief from expenditure incurred in marriage, but breach of the rules of marriage is dealt with severely and the defaulters are heavily punished. The financial burden imposed on erring individuals, as said earlier, is enormous. Thus, very few Hill Korwa, dare to violate the rule.

Old age

Old age is no excuse for idleness. Birjhoo, ninety years old former Lotadar of Biria who raised a Korwa batallion to fight against the Nagesia rebels at Samripath (District Surguja) on behest of the erstwhile ruler of Surguja in 1920 was found felling trees with axe and bringing fuel for domestic use in spite of his physical infirmity and semi-blindness.

An active old male member in the household gets a higher status and dominates its affairs. The power of decision making in day-to day affairs of the household rests on him.

It will however, be wrong to assume that only the active olds are well looked after. Even the invalid are not neglected either by members of the family or the society at large. An epileptic and semi-lunatic in Sardapath and a blind in Rakaiya were looked after properly by their brother and brother's son respectively.

Old men and women keep themselves busy with their grand children giving badly needed respite to the lady of the house. Old women excell themselves in midwifery because of their thorough knowledge about the local herbs and are very much sought after not only by the members of their own tribe but also by other tribes living in the area. Such women contribute the remuneration they receive from the profession to the earning of the household. In most of the cases remuneration given to an old lady is a *dhoti* (loin cloth) or Rs. 2/- in lieu of it.

In serious matters like marriage negotiations,sale of land etc., opinion of the elders is sought and given full weight by the youngers. Nadi's father died in Rakaiya leaving behind a small piece of land which was to be distributed among the three sons. Further fragmentation of the land might have rendered it uneconomic. Hence, Nadi sought the advice of his father's younger brother as how to distribute the land among the three brothers. The old man advised Nadi to sell the land and distribute money in three equal parts. Thus, a simmering crisis amongst the three brothers was amicably averted.

Some old people assumed the role of Sayana at intra-village and inter-village level and participated actively in the *jat-panchayat* and played a key role in the Korwa authority structure.

An old widowed mother and widower father is looked after by their sons. The old father derives his authority from ownership of the family landholding and is properly looked after even if the land has already been transferred in his son's name. The old receive a pair of clothes from their children every year.

The last journey

Death is the will of God as Ronha of Rakaiya had put it : "It (life) is His *kheti* (farming). He may keep one alive or may take one's life back".

When a person dies, all clan members assemble. A separate leaf hut (*koomba*) is erected for giving a bath to the dead body. In case of a man's death his body is given bath by the deceased's male relatives. Young boys and girls are not allowed to enter inside the *koomba* where bath is given. When a woman dies, the female members of her family bathe the dead body.

After bath the dead body is wrapped in a single piece of cloth three feet wide and nine feet long. It is called *kapphan*. Then each member of the deceased's clan and his co-villagers pour a few drops of water in the mouth of the deceased. This is done on the assumption that the people might have dere-licted from the duties in looking after the person well when he was alive. Now, in order to compensate for their failure in attending him, they supply water to the dead.

A bier is made by putting two parallel bamboo poles and a number of bamboo strips horizontally fastened with them by bark ropes. Simultaneously a chest deep grave (*dhotha*) 2 feet in width and 6½ feet in length is dug for laying the body at rest. The graveyard is usually situated outside the village boundary. The body is taken to the graveyard (*murghat*) by male members of the deceased clan. After laying the body at rest, personal belonging of the deceased are also put beside the body. The Baiga of the village where the death has occurred throws a handful of soil inside the grave first. Then others follow him in throwing mud till the pit is levelled. A few stones are put on the grave as a sign of indentification.

A basket containing about 3 kgs of foodgrains is put beside the grave. The personal effects of the dead and food grains are kept with a view that the dead might need them in his next life.

Women dying during pregnancy or of small-pox are believed to become evil spirits. In such cases the dead are not buried but cremated as it is believed that the spirit of the dead may come out from the grave and harass the people.

After burying the dead the people return to the village from the *marghat* through a different route because it is believed that if the path of the dead (*mua ka rasta*) *is followed,* there will be repetition of death in the village.

Hearth is not commissioned for five days in the house of the bereaved as a sign of mourning. During this period food is supplied by members of the lineage viz., brothers living separately, paternal uncles or their sons. Pending the performance of *kamun,* the purificatory bath taken by members of the clan and co-villagers of the deceased all socio-economic activities of the bereaved family come to a standstill.

Kamun

kamun is observed on 5th, 7th, 9th or 11th day after the death. The period is decided after reviewing the age and status of the deceased. When a child dies, *kamun* is performed on the 5th day. At the death of an adolescence, *kamun* is performed on the 7th day. In case of an adult the bath is taken on the 9th day and for an old *kamun* takes place on the 11th day. It may be noted from the number of days that all of them are odd numbers. Even number have not been prescribed as it is feared that there will be repetition of death in the family. On the day of *kamun,* members of the clan, affines, and Mukhyas of all Korwa villages under the jurisdiction of a Lotadar assemble at the house where death has occurred. The participants shave each other's head reciprocally by the help of an arrow head. After the hair-cut, the people have bath in the nearby pool. The head of the bereaved family offers oil to all participants. Then the Lotadar raises a pitcher filled with liquor (*daroo*) by both of his hands and addresses the gathering in the following words: Eh ghar ma haran maran ho gai, ee man jal liya nahin. In logan ka sagaa ma samilkarat hain. (Death has occurred in this house, the members of the bereaved household have not taken water. I reunite these people with their kinsmen).

Death causes pollution leading to a temporary separation of the bereaved from the rest of the tribe. The Lotadar, thus re-unites the polluted members of the tribe into its fold. The ritual of re-union is followed by the *kamun* feast. The articles of food served in the feast consist of rice and lantil. A piece of mutton or pork is also put on the heap of rice. After meal the participants are offered *handi*. The poorer families usually do not serve meals to the participants but offer *handi*.

A slight variation in *kamun* rituals has been observed at Sardapath and Maltipur where the office of the Lotadar now does not exist. In these villages the Mukhya or in his absence, a Sayana raises the *lota*, for re-unification of members of the polluted household.

Social Organisation

As already indicated, Korwa are divided into two major segments viz., the Pahari Korwa (Hill Korwa) and the Dih/Danr/Dehari Korwa (Plain dwelling Korwa). The Hill Korwa, as their name implies, live on the top of hillocks generally covered by forests in dispersed settlements. Their economy is based on a combination of hunting, food gathering, a rude form of agriculture, and wage labour. In the past the people practised shifting cultivation. Between the two segments the Hill Korwa are considered socio-ritually inferior to the plain Korwa as the former eat carrion and beef. The only Hindu caste maintaining *jajmani* relations with the Hill Korwa is the Ghasia, who are professional drummers and dancers and are invited to perform their dancing feats during any wedding in a Hill Korwa household.

The Dih Korwa live in big villages side by side with the other tribes of the area. They live in clustered settlements and follow agricultural pursuits. They are unable to recollect if they were ever shifting cultivators. The Dih Korwa observe commensal taboos with the Hill Korwa and do not accept cooked food from the later. Raw tobacco (*khaini*), *handi* and *jagra* beer are, however, accepted. Inter-marriage between the two groups is nearly absent. Castes maintaining *jajmani* ties with the Dih Korwa are Brahmin (Katta), the Barber (Thakur) and Washerman (Dhobi). The Dih Korwa's economy is not as dependent on forest as that of the Hill Korwa. The Dih Korwa are good agriculturists like the neighbouring Oraon, Kawar, and Nagesia.

The Hill Korwa are patrilineal and patrilocal. Descent, inheritance, and succession are traced through the male line. The tribe is divided into a number of clans, which are Kuri or Goti. These units are further sub-divided into a number of *bhaiyars*. The *bhaiyars* are composed of a number of families that trace their descent to a genealogically establishes common ancestor.

Kuri or Goti is an exogamous unit consisting of unilineal descent group the membership to which is determined through father's line.

The four villages under study are multi-clan villages. Some of the important Korwa clans found in these villages are Hasadwar, Edigwar, Murihar, Samadwar, and Ginumwar.

Origin of Clans

The origin of clans is explained by the following myth. "Once upon a time when the division of Korwa population into smaller segments took place, those who erected their hearth (*chulha*) by mud (*hasad*) were called Hasadwar; those who erected their hearth with the help of stones plastered it with human excreta, were named Edigwar; those who killed dogs with the help of their bows and arrows, beheaded them and erected hearths with the heads of dogs (*muri*) were called Murihar. Some of them killed deer and erected hearths by deer heads were called Samadwar. The most inefficient in hunting caught *gina* fish with their hands and were known as Ginumawar".

Members of Samadwar clan live in the northeastern part of the Surguja District near Jonkapath hills. The population of

Ginumawar is localised in Udaipur Tehsil of Raigarh District. The Hasadwar, Murihar and Edigwar are evenly distributed in Surguja and Raigarh Districts.

The Table no. 2.6 shows distribution of population according to clans.

Toble 6 shows that Hasadwar is the mostly represented clan to be followed by Edigwar, Murihar, Samadwar and Ginumwar. The latter are evenly distributed in Maltipur, Bansajhal and Sardapath. This clan is absent in other villages. The population of the Ginumwar mostly consist of the female who are brought from Udaipur (Raigarh District) through marriage or children whose biological father belonged to the Ginumwar clan and who came to live with their mothers in the household of their respective step-fathers.

The three clans Hasadwar, Edigwar, and Murihar constitute 95.24 per cent of the Hill Korwa population in the 4 villages under study.

Functions of Clan

The most important function of a clan is regulation of marriage rules among its members. Breach of marriage regulation provokes it to act and punish the offenders. On occasions of a mourning, members of the clan pool their resources to enable a poor family in arranging *kamun* feast. Clan affiliation of a girl does not change with her marriage. In general it is traced through the male line.

Manhar of Malitpur, a member of Hasadwar clan, married a widow whose previous husband belonged to Edigwar clan. She became pregnant along with two children to live with her new husband. Four months after marriage she gave birth to a female child. As a matter of rule the girl should have belonged to Edigwar clan but she was stated to have belonged to her step-father's clan. When asked about this anomaly, Sukkhan of Maltipur explained: "A woman can never be trusted. She can withstand hunger for food but cannot stand the hunger of *sammai* (vagina). Invariably she goes out in deep forest for collection of fuel and can be conceived by any one who

TABLE 2.6

Distribution of Population According to Clans

Names of Villages	Hasad-war	Percent-age	Edigwar	Percent-age	Murihar	Percent-age	Samad-war	Percent-age	Ginumwar	Percent-age	Total Popu-lation
Rakaiya	34	23.61	58	40.28	32	22.22	20	13.89	—	—	144
Maltipur	110	62.86	28	16.00	32	18.29	—	—	5	2.85	175
Bansajhal	96	47.76	78	38.81	19	9.75	—	—	8	3.98	201
Sardapath	160	49.85	152	47.35	2	0.62	—	—	7	2.18	321
Total	400	47.56	316	37.57	85	10.11	20	2.38	20	2.38	841

mounts on her. A woman does not feel satisfied even by ten persons. Who knows whose *bija* (seed) she carries in her *udar* (belly)? Her children thus should be included in the clan of the person with whom she marries and lives as a wife". It was rather an exceptional case. All children do not change their clan affiliation after their mother's re-marriage with a man belonging to different clans. Usually, clan affiliation of step-children differs from the step-father's clan affiliation.

In case, a man dies issueless his property is inherited by his father's elder brother or the children of father's elder brother, or by the father's younger brother or his children. If there is none in the above category of relatives, the property goes to the nearest relatives belonging to the Bhaiyar of the deceased. If no such person exists, it goes to the nearest relative belonging to the clan of the deceased. In any case the property belonging to a particular clan is not allowed to pass on to any other clan.

Members of clan help to build a house for their newly marrieds. Biphna of Rakaiya decided to build a new house after the arrival of his first issue. His father Sukkhan, with whom he shared the house earlier, gave him a piece of land adjacent to his house for construction of a new house. Soon construction of the house started and the male members belonging to Sukkhan's clan came to the site of construction, saw the house in progress, gave their comments, and returned. Sukkhan felt annoyed due to unhelpful attitude of his clan members, who also complained that Sukkhan thought to build the house all by himself and did not ask the members of his clan for any assistance. They decided therefore to stay away. Realising his fault Sukkhan apologised to the *sayanas*. The next day all male members belonging to Sukkhan's clan were seen at the construction site helping him in building the house.

Bhaiyar

A Bhaiyar, as alrady stated consist of persons having a common male ancestor. This social unit may be considered as the lineage. Marriage within Bhaiyar is strictly prohibited. No case of marriage within the group came into notice during investigations. The Bhaiyar relationships are referred to as Bhaiyary. Members of a Bhaiyar do not necessarily live in the same village and sometimes are scattered in a number of villages. Members living in far off villages know little about their Bhaiyars living in other villages. The usual occasion of meeting the members of the Bhaiyar living in nearby villages is after harvest, when *handi* is brewed in every Korwa household and members of the unit exchange visit. Marriage, mourning, and *kamun* or other similar occasions bring members of a Bhaiyar together. The members of a Bhaiyar living in the same village fight unitedly for asserting their rights with members of other lineage in matters of land or marriage disputes. Members of a lineage depend on each other to meet crises developing from time to time in the life cycle. A sudden death leaves the bereaved family in economic crisis. The family looks upon members of the Bhaiyar for assistance which the latter readily extend. Sometimes members of lineage exchange bullocks with one another for carrying out agricultural operations. Small loans of money and food grains are also exchanged between members of a lineage whenever such necessity arises.

Household

A Korwa household consists of an individual, his wife, children, parents and unmarried sisters. All members of a household get their meals from one pot (*ek handi ke khawaiya*). The head of the family is called the *gharmuar* and enjoys unchallenged authority over members of his household. He represents his family on all collective occasions of social, religious, economic and political nature in day to day life of the village. He receives from members of his household maximum respect, obedience, and cooperation. The economic functions of a *gharmuar* are to organise and regulate economic activities. He is responsible to provide livelihood to each member of the household. The income of individual members of a household is pooled with him through which he sees that each member of the household gets his needs fulfilled. If he is incapable of doing so, the household unit breaks into smaller units having their own respective heads. Hence the existence of a household largely depends on the capability of its head (*gharmuar*).

The nature of composition of households assorted into various types has been given in Table 2.7

Nascent households

Nascent household consists of a couple without any issue of their own or adopted. Phool Singh of Sardapath married a woman who died of small pox after seven years of marriage without bearing any issue. Soon after Phool Singh remarried but this time also did not get any issue from his second wife. There are 9 Nascent households in our study samples, 4 in Bansajhal and 5 in Sardapath.

Nuclear households

In a Nuclear household the couple live with their unmarried children. The frequency of Nuclear households is the highest in all the four villages under study. Out of 149 households, 59 are of nuclear type. Rakaiya has 21 nuclear households out of 30, Maltipur has 5 out of 23, Bansajhal has 8 out of 36 and Sardapath has 25 out of 60 nuclear households.

Lineally extended households

Such households consist of a married couple and their married children. Each married couple has a separate partition to live under the same roof. Meals, however, are served from a common hearth.

Sukkhan of Rakaiya lived with his wife Jugni and unmarried younger daughter, Budli. His eldest widowed daughter Mahuari also lived there with a three year old son Chamru who was the heir of his deceased father's land. Mahuari was the custodian and keeper of her son's property. Chamru's father's land was cultivated by the younger brother of his deceased father Lagni, on the basis of share-cropping. The income Mahuari gets from her deceased husband's land was sufficient to look after Chamru. She advanced small sums of money to her kinsmen against mortgage of their land. Mahuari did not remarry because of her apprehensions that in case of remarriage she will loose the benefits of her late husband's land. She

TABLE 2.7

Distribution of Korwa Households

	No. of household	Nascent household	Nuclear household	Paternally Extended household	Horizontally Extended Household	Other types	Broken household
	(%)	(%)	(%)	(%)	(%)	(%)	(%)
Rakaiya	30 (100.00)	-	21 (70.00)	8 (26.67)	1 (3.33)	-	-
Maltipur	23	-	5 (21.74)	6 (26.09)	-	11 (47.82)	1 (4.35)
Bansajhal	36	4 (11.11)	8 (22.22)	9 (25.00)	1 (2.78)	14 (38.89)	
Sardapath	60	5 (8.33)	25 (41.67)	11 (18.34)	6 (10.00)	9 (15.00)	4 (6.66)
Total	149	9 (6.04)	59 (39.60)	34 (22.82)	8 (5.37)	34 (22.82)	5 (3.35)

was not sure whether, in such case she would be able to keep her son along with her new husband. She was contributing regularly to her father Sukkhan towards meeting the expenses of her meals. Biphina, Sukkhan's son was also living in the same house with his wife Bihini. Sukkhan's next daughter Chuli was living in the same house with her husband Manager, as *gharjawain.*

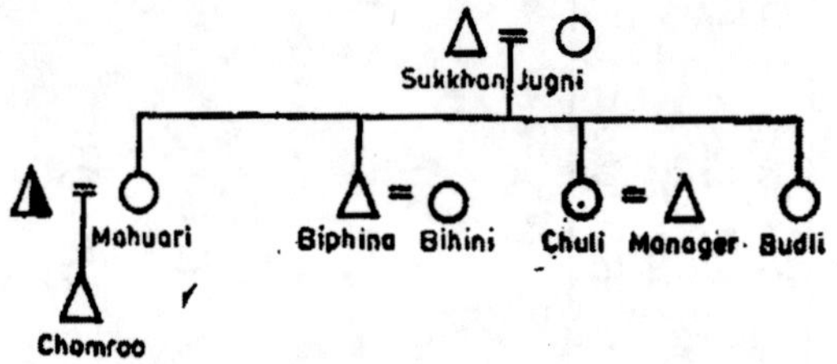

Diagram : 2.3

The diagram here represents the units just described.

Sukkhan is the *ghar-maur.* The four units live under the same roof and are served from the same *chulha* (hearth). Biphina (unit 3) and Manager (unit 2) were working as agricultural labourers and used to get one day's leave after every nine working days in order to cultivate Sukkhan's land. The cash earned by two men is pooled with Sukkhan in order to purchase a bullock in future. Sukkhan was responsible for the maintenance of his own wife, his son's wife, daughter and her husband, and an unmarried younger daughter.

There are 34 such households in which parents live with their married as well as unmarried children. In Rakaiya, Maltipur, Bansajhal, and Sardapath the number of vertically extended households was found 8, 6, 9 and 11 per cent respectively.

Laterally extended households

Such households contain ego, his wife and children, his married brothers, their wives and children and his unmarried siblings. The married brothers live under the same roof but in different portions of the house and eat from their respective *chulha* (hearth) while the unmarried siblings get their food from the ego's or some other brothers' *chulha.* All the brothers toil collectively as according to revenue regulations sometimes land is not transferable.

The household diagram of Muna Ram of Sardapath may be taken as specimen of this type.

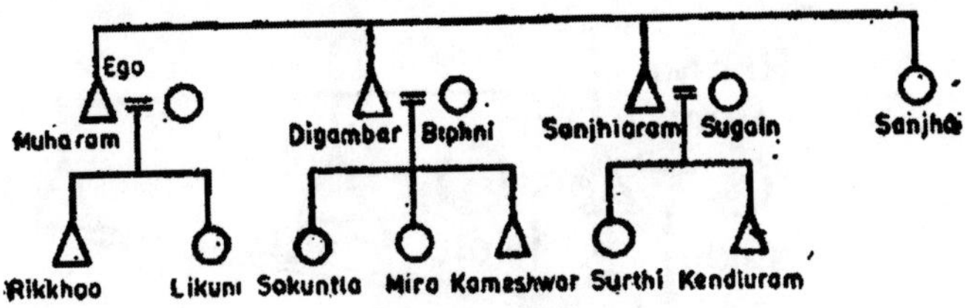

Diagram : 2.4

Muna Ram had two younger brothers and a sister. The two brothers were married and had children. Their sister, Sanjaho, 11 years was unmarried and was getting her meals from Muna Ram's *chulha.* Muna Ram's two younger brothers, Digamber and Sanjhia Ram, had their separate *chulhas* but were living in the same house. There are eight households of this type. Rakaiya has one, Bansajhal one and Sardapath has six.

Polygynous households

This type of household is composed of ego, his multiple spouses, and children from each wife. The number of spouses in this type of household was found to be two in 94.12 per cent cases and the tree in 5.88 per cent cases.

Ronha Ram of Sardapath was keeping three wives at a time. His household diagram is furnished below.

Ronha Ram's three wives, Baisakhi, Noli, and Chikli were living in separate apartments. Baisakhi had two sons and Noli had a daughter. Baisakhi was called by her husband as Barki (the senior), the next Majhalki and youngest Chotki. Majhalki used to call Baisakhi Didi and was so-called by Chotki. Barki was responsible for allocation of the day-to-day household duties. Food gathering activities were, however, done collectively. Nearly 11 per cent of the total households were polygynous in composition. Maltipur had 13.04 per cent of them, Bansajhal had 25.00 per cent and Sardapath had 8.33 per cent.

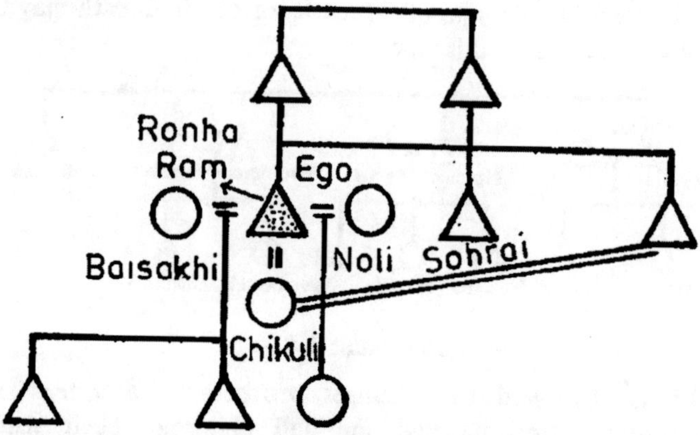

Diagram : 2.5

Other types

Other types of households are stated below:

1. Ego, his two wives, their children, ego's brother and his children, and ego's widowed mother.

The following diagram shows the households composition of Sonha of Maduasarai (Maltipur).

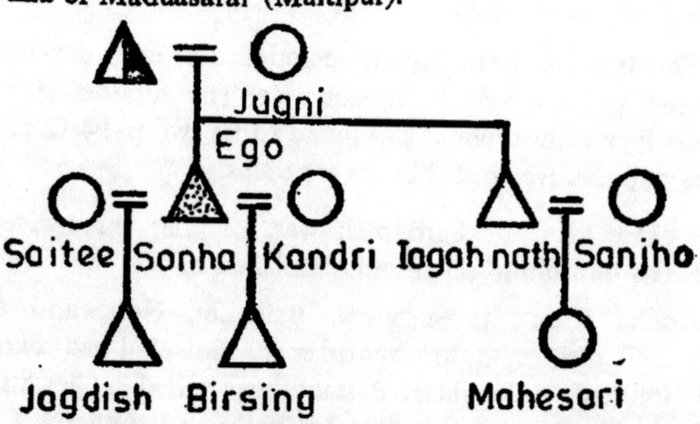

Diagram: 2.6

2. Ego, his wife and children, his mother and step-mother.

Following is the household diagram of Surta of Bansajhal representing the above subtype.

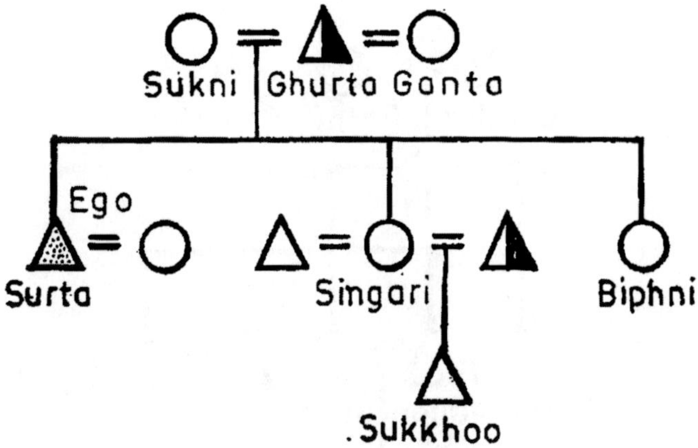

Diagram : 2.7

In the above diagram Surta was found living with his own mother Sukri and step-mother Ganta. Surta's father Ghurta died leaving her step-mother issueless. His younger sister Singar was a widow with a son Sukkhoo. But she remarried and left his son behind with her elder brother.

3. Ego with or without his wife, his son, son's multiple spouses and their children.

The household diagram of Chadra Patel of Maltipur is given on the next base as a representative specimen of the subtype.

In is shown in the diagram 2.8 that Chadra's son Dhansai married first Kundro and had two sons Mangal and Kolai. Subsequently he remarried his first wife's younger sister Gundli and had two daughters from her, named Poti and Kuli. Chadra's daughter was married in Dorhadih but her husband deserted her and remarried. She returned to her father with a son Jugroo and was remarried shortly. She left her son with her father.

4. Ego, his wives and children and his brother's multiple wives and a widowed mother.

The following household diagram of Bir Sai of Maltipur is a representative specimen of the above subtype.

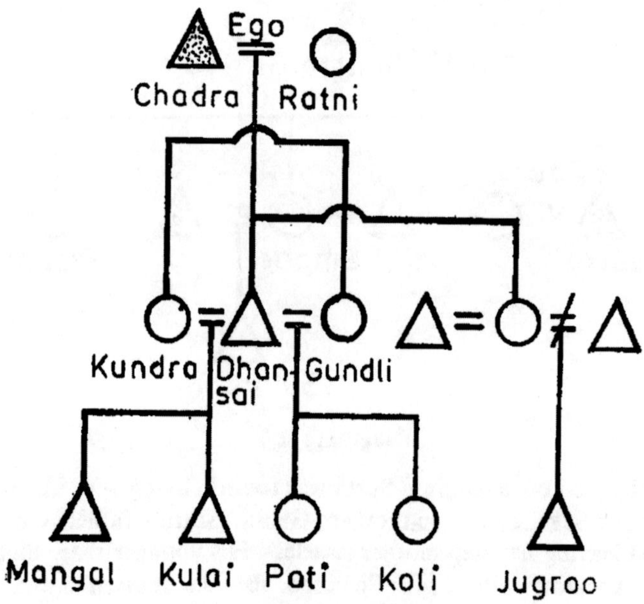

Diagram : 2.8

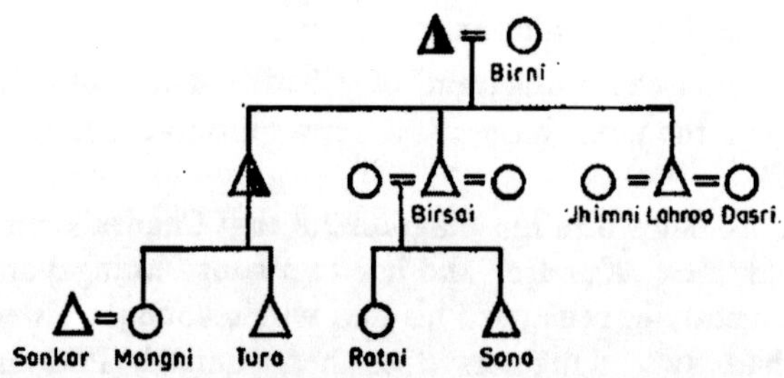

Diagram: 2.9

It is shown in the above diagram that Bir Sai had two wives at a time. He had two children from the first wife and the second wife was issueless. His widowed mother Birni was also living with him. His deceased elder brother left behind his daughter Mangani and a son Tura, who were also living with Bir Sai. Mangani was married with Sankar of Darhidanr village but was living with her father's younger brother. Her husband was a *gharjawain*. The younger brother of Bir Sai, Lahroo first married Jhimini of Vhipar Kaya village and then subsequently he married Dasri of Amadarhi village. He has no issue from either of the two wives.

There are 34 polygynous households in Maltipur, 14 in Bansajhal, and 9 in Sardapath. The higher incidence of polygyny in the three above mentioned villages may be attributed to their relatively better economy. The above villages have bigger average landholdings when compared with Rakaiya which does not show any polygynous union.

5. Sukhna of Maltipur was looking after the children of his step-mother and her previous husband. Though the two sons of his step-mother Chander and Locha were not related to him by blood and belonged to a different clan, Sukha was responsible for their maintenance and was behaving with them as if his own brothers. The following diagram depicts the composition of the household.

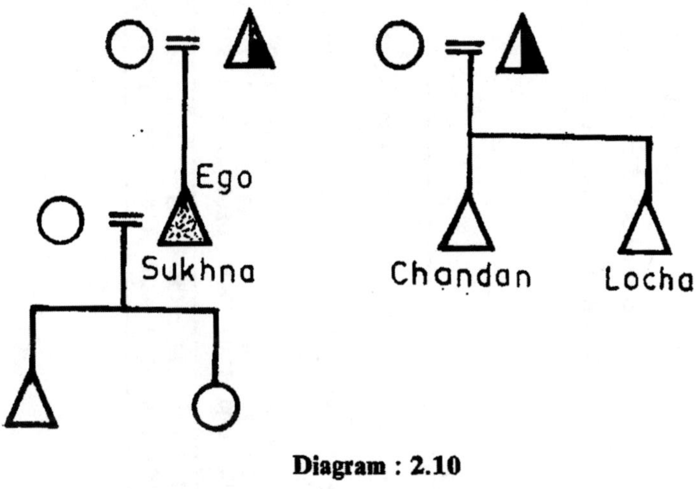

Diagram : 2.10

6. Doenga of Maltipur was living with his wife, his children and his wife's widowed mother, his own sons, their wives, and children.

7. Masomatin of Sardapath, a widow, was living with her daughters and a son.

TABLE 2.8

Households Size According to Members

Villages	NUMBER OF HOUSEHOLDS ACCORDING TO MEMBERS													
	1	2	3	4	5	6	7	8	9	10	11	12	13	14	Total No. of House-holds
Rakaiya	—	—	5	13	5	2	2	1	2	—	—	—	—	—	30
Percentage	—	—	16.67	43.33	16.67	6.67	6.67	3.33	6.66	—	—	—	—	—	100.00
Maltipur	—	—	2	1	3	2	2	3	4	1	2	—	2	1	23
Percentage	—	—	8.70	4.34	13.04	8.70	8.70	13.04	17.39	4.34	8.70	—	8.70	4.34	100.00
Bansajhal	—	2	5	3	6	0	4	5	—	—	2	—	—	—	36
Percentage	—	5.56	13.84	8.33	16.66	25.00	11.11	13.89	—	—	5.56	—	—	—	100.00
Sardapath	1	5	6	9	11	12	7	7	—	1	—	—	—	1	60
Percentage	1.67	8.32	10.00	15.00	18.33	20.00	11.67	11.67	—	1.67	—	—	—	1.67	100.00
Total	1	7	18	26	25	25	15	16	6	2	4	—	2	2	149
Percentage	0.67	4.70	12.08	17.45	16.78	16.78	10.07	10.74	4.03	1.34	2.68	—	1.34	1.34	100.00

8. Sukhi of Sardapath, an aged widow, was living alone. She owned her father's landholding, the size of which was 27 acres. She gave her land to a Mahto on sharecropping. The ratio of households mentioned in type 8 is 3.35 per cent. In Maltipur it is 4.35 per cent and in Sardapath 6.67 per cent.

Household size

The size of Korwa households varies between 1 and 14. The households having 3 to 8 members constitute the majority. The ratio of such houses is 83.89 per cent. Nearly 11 per cent of the households have between 9 and 14 members. There is a single house with a lone member and there are 7 houses with 2 members who in general are married issueless couple. The average Hill Korwa household has 5.7 members. Households size in Kakaiya ranges between 3 and 9, in Maltipur between 3 and 14 in Bansajhal between 2 and 11. The range is widest at Sardapath, between 1 and 14. There is no household in any of the villages having 12 members. Economic restraints in Rakaiya seem to have reduced the size of households. Maltipur and Sardapath are almost at par and Bansajhal comes in between.

Residence after marriage

A Korwa girl leaves her family of orientation after her marriage and stays with her husband which may be termed as her family of procreation. *Gharjawain* or uxorilocal families are an exception in which a man does not part with his daughter even after her marriage. The daughter lives within the house of her father. The usual pattern of her husband residence after marriage is patrilocal.

Inheritance of property

Property among the Hill Korwa may be divided into two broad categories, movable and immovable. (a) Movable property consists of bows, arrows, clothes, ornaments, utensils, musical instruments, cattle, ploughs and other household effects. (b) Immovable property comprises land, house etc.

When a person dies, his bows, arrows and the utensils of personal use are buried with him. Ornaments and clothes of a deceased woman are equally divided amongst her daughters and daughters-in-law. Personal savings and cattle are divided equally among sons.

A Korwa individual, according to *mitakshara* school of Hindu Law is entitled to claim the partition of immovable property in the life-time of his father but the latter remains the *dejure* owner of the property. Ownership in such cases may be considered as joint between the father and sons. A man can become *dejure* owner of the immovable property only after the death of his father or if the latter transfers the ownership to his son by an act of will. Equal shares are given to all male heirs. Women are not entitled to any share of their father's property. A willing father, however, can give a portion of land to his daughter. This happens invariably in case of *gharjawain* marriages. In such cases when a woman is the owner of property, the property is inherited by her sons and never by her husband unless she has left a will in this regard.

When a person informally divides his landed property among his sons, usually he keeps a portion of land for himself and his minor sons, if any. In a polygynous household male chidren from different wives inherit equal portions of their father's property.

Duties and Privileges of Members of a Household

Husband and wife are equal partners in the maintenance of their children. The former is responsible to satisfy various needs of the latter and in return, receives latter's co-operation in all household pursuits. The husband goes for hunting or to his fields or to *grihat* for labour. The wife goes to the forest for collection of forest produces, or grazing the cattle. On market days she accompanies her husband to market for small purchases and enjoys drinking *daru* with him.

Parents are responsible for upbringing of children and children contribute their bit by attending their younger siblings, killing small games, and bringing small loads of fire wood and leaves from the forest. In an extended household, the duty of the maintenance of old parents lies primarily on married sons. Step-mothers pass their widowhood in the house of their step-sons in case they do not have their own children to look after. Similarly step-siblings are properly looked after and not discriminated.

Kinship System

Members of the tribe are closely knit with one another through various bonds of kinship and refer to each other by extending a set of kinship terms. These terms indicate and manifest a set of behaviours. The most important kin are the consanguinal and affinal one.

Consanguinal bonds exist between members of ascending and descending generations through the father while affinal relations exist between ego and his wife and all relations linked through marriage.

The Korwa kinship terminology may be divided into two categories as under:

(a) Classificatory

(b) Denotative

Classificatory system may be termed as the ascribed system of kinship terminology of the Korwa while denotative terms have come through borrowing from the neighbouring ethnic groups. The changes in some of classificatory kinship terms and their splitting into denotative terms as a result of borrowing have been shown in the Table 2.9.

It is evident from this table that the term 'Gungoo' and 'Korian' do not differentiate sex and generation of the referred kin whereas the borrowed terms *bara* and *bari* differentiate the criterion of sex. A majority of Korwa kinship terms fall in the category of classificatory kinship terminology.

Examples are furnished below :

TABLE 2.9

Changes in Korwa Kinship Terminology

Relationship	Traditional Classificatory Kinship terms	Borrowed Kinship terms
Da So	Korain	Nati
Da Da		Natini
So So		Nati
So Da		Natini
Fa el Br	Gungoo	Bara
Fa el Br Wi		Bari
Fa Fa el Br Wi		Bari
Wi Si So		Bara
Wi Si Da		Bari
Yo Br So		Bara
Hu Br So		"
Fa Fa Fa		"
So So So		"
Hu Br Da		Bari
Fa Fa Mo		"
So So Da		"

Gungoo is used for: Fa Fa Fa, Fa Fa Mo, So So So, So So So Da, Fa Fa Br So, Fa Fa Br Da, Fa el Br, Fa el Br Wi, Br So, Br Da, Br So So, Br So Da, Mo Si Hu, Wi Si So and Wi Si Hu.

Aja is the term for: Fa Fa, Mo Fa, Fa Fa Br. Mo Fa Br, Fa Fa Si Hu, Hu Mo Fa, Wi Mo Fa, Hu Fa Fa, Wi Fa Fa.

Aji is the term for: Fa Mo, Mo Mo. Fa Fa Br Wi, Wi Fa Br Wi, Wi Fa Mo and Wi Mo Mo.

Mama is used for: Mo Br, Hu Mo Br, Wi Mo Br, Hu Fa Si Hu, Fa Si Hu, Si Hu Fa, Br Wi Fa.

Mami is used for: Fa Si, Hu Fa Si, Wi Fa Si, Mo Br Wi, Hu Mo Br Wi, Wi Mo Bo Wi, Fa Fa Br Da, Wi Fa Fa Br Da, Hu Mo Mo Br Da and Wi Mo Br Da.

Korwa kinship terminology shows the prevalence of cross-cousin marriage. Mo Br Wi, Fa Si, and Wi Mo are referred as Mami. The people observe the rule of teknonymy and by virtue of that they do not have any term of address for their wives. This rule seems to have been extended to Mo Br Da and Fa Si Da who are potential mates. Therefore, they do not address each other by extending any kinship term.

A few denotative terms have been described in the following table.

TABLE 2.10

Korwa Kinship Terminology

Terms of Kinship	Terms of Reference	Terms of Address	Remark
1	2	3	4
Father (Fa)	Apan	Dau, baba	
Mother (Mo)	Aya	Aya	
Husband (Hu)	'dau' of so-and-so, loga	No term	Teknonymy
Wife (Wi)	No term	No term	-do-
Father's younger Brother (Fa yo Br)	Pitya kaka	Kaka	
Fa yo Br Wi	Kaki	Kaki	
Mo Si	Kaki	Kaki	
Mo Si Hu	Kaka	Kaka	
Hu el Br	Bhasur	No term	Avoidance
Hu el Br Wi	Derh-sais	Derh-sais	-do-
Wi yo Br	Sara	Sara, babu	
Wi el Si	Derh-sais	No term	-do-
Hu yo Br	Deur	by name babu	Joking
Mo Br	Mama	No term	
Mo Br Wi	Mami	Mami	
yo Br Wi	Lainkoo-Bhawa	No term	Avoidance

1	2	3	3
Hu Br Wi	Hilly	Hilly	Joking
Fa Si	Mami	Mami	-do-
Fa Si Hu	Mama	Mama	
Mo el Si	Bari	Bari	
Mo el Si Hu	Bara	Bara	
So Wi	mini	kiBahuria	
Step son	Kath-beta	No term	Descriptive
Step father	Kaka	No term	
Step daughter	Kath-beti	No term	
Step mother	Kaki	Kaki	

The cousin terminology of the Hill Korwa contains no terms of reference or address for cross cousins whereas the parallel cousins are equated terminologically with siblings. Cross cousin marriage is a prescribed form of marriage. Hence Mo Br Da and Fa Si Da are considered as potential mates. The rule of teknonymy is mainly responsible for absence of kinship terms of cross cousins. The cousin terminology of the Hill Korwa does not fit in any of the six types described by Murdock.[3] It is nearest to Mundari.[4]

Husband-Wife

The conjugal life of a couple starts after *mangabara.* No sooner a bride enters in the family of procreation she becomes an active partner in socio-economic pursuits of her husband's households. If the husband comes with a handful of grains, she gets herself busy in dehusking them and cooking meal for him. Upbringing of children is their collective responsibility. The wife is responsible for carrying out the daily chores, whereas the husband is for procuring means of livelihood. A Korwa woman keeps herself busy with husking lever, in cleaning the house and utensils, washing clothes, fetching water from the nearby stream, cooking and taking care of the tiny kitchen garden attached to her house. As soon as the husband enters into the house, he takes over the function of looking after children from his wife sparing her for cooking. A pregnant Korwa woman does not cook due to pollution.

In case there are no other female members in the family, the husband himself cooks and provides meals to his wife and children. Even when a couple grow old, their mutual responsibilities toward one another remain unchanged. They sometimes live in a separate house, away from their married sons and help each other in socio-economic pursuits of their own household. The two are equal partners in eking out a livelihood for themselves and other dependent members of the household. She is invariably consulted by her husband in all important matters pertaining to the family.

In polygynous households the first wife assumes the role of manager, supervising the socio-economic activities of her juniors.

Husband and wife relationship in the Korwa society is marked with the sense of co-operation, mutual adjustment, tolerance, and trust. Children are joint responsibility of the two. The wife is, thus, an equal partner of her husband in all thick and thin of life and day-to-day socio-economic pursuits of the household.

Father and Son

The very foundation of household economy and solidarity in the patrilineal Korwa society is based on filial ties. The son is an active contributor to household earnings from his early childhood. A father equips his young son with a small bow made of bamboo stave and bark string and arrows made from spokes of bicycle wheel for aiming at small birds and fruits and with a small axe by which he cuts low and tender branches of trees and returns home with a small bundle of fire wood.

During a dance performance Rakaiya, Kolha, six year old son of Bajroo insisted on playing a *mandar* (drum). Bajroo asked other children to part with their tiny drums, but none obliged him. In the meantime the child started crying and Bajroo disappeared from the scene for a while and returned with a small imitation of *mandar*. The drum was made by cutting a small piece of cylindrical wood and its both sides were covered with green leaves fastened by bark stripes fitted with a long bark rope tied from both sides of the drum for holding the instrument by neck. The child was satisfied to get what he wanted and soon he was seen beating his imitation drum along with other children.

When a boy attains the age seven or eight years, he becomes the caretaker of the household cattle and takes them to forest for grazing. In the 9th or 10th year of his age, he starts working in his father's field. Ploughing is usually done by those children who can control the draft animals easily under their paternal supervision.

Dereliction from duty towards the family pursuits invites wrath of the father on his son.

Ten year old Bhola of Rakaiya was once repeatedly asked by his father Sukura to go for ploughing but the boy did not pay any heed. Infuriated Sukura gave a thrashing to his son and led him forcibly to the field.

As soon as a boy finds out a suitable girl for him the vigilant father comes to know about it with a sense of satisfaction blended with pride. He tries to settle the marriage through the services of a mediator and incurs all marriage expenses of his son. After marriage the father tries to keep the couple with him till the son expresses a desire to live separately. When separated, the father helps him building a new house foı his son. Separation of a househould in Korwa society is a natural phenomenon. A Korwa father, not only helps his son in his marriage but does his best in getting him settled.

An old Korwa father does not depend entirely on his son and discharges his duties as a supervisor and head of the household. He warns his son (s) repeatedly about the immediate tasks to be performed in the household.

The son in return is supposed to be righteous, obedient, co-operative, and hard working. He should be efficient enough to share his father's burdens for smooth running of the household.

Dispute between the two were nearly non-existent among the Hill Korwa. Even under influence of liquor, the son maintains a distance form his father. The two never go inside a *bhatti* together for consumption of liquor. A Korwa father always talks proudly of his son. His son's expertise in archery and qualities of an efficient conversationalist with the outsiders etc., are his favourite topics in conversation.

Harya Ram of Sardapath was a proud father of his son Baisakhoo, who, as Harya Ram claimed, was the only Korwa possessing Fitter's certificate from Industrial Training Institute, Raigarh. At the same time, Harya Ram was equally worried due to his son's inability to get a suitable job.

A Korwa boy begins marginal economic pursuits from an early age of 5 or 6 years mostly in the company of his father. He becomes an active partner of his father in agricultural activities by the time he attains the age of 10 years. Thus most of his time is passed in father's company which helps to strengthen his emotional attachment with his father. The warmth of father-son relationship is deeper than the mother-son relationship. It does not however, imply that mother's role is insignificant in the upbringing of her son. She provides every possible comfort to him so long she does not change the husband. But most of the Korwa women change husbands twice or thrice during their life time. Some of them have been found to change husbands five times. In case of remarriage of a Korwa woman, the daughters from earlier husbands move with the mother whereas sons are left behind with their father and paternal relatives.

The payment of bride-price make a male issue an economic liability for a Korwa mother and step-father. A daughter on the other hand is considered an asset because she fetches bride-price to her mother and step-father. This may be the reason for women leaving their sons behind and taking their daughters away from their divorced husbands. When the son accompanies his mother to his step-father's house he starts losing parental affection and slowly his position in the family is reduced to that of a domestic servant. This fact is resented by the patri-kin of the boy. If the father of such an unfortunate boy dies, he is looked after by his grandfather. The grand parents, in such cases never allow their grand-children specially, grandsons to live with their mother after her remarriage.

Koka of Rakaiya was murdered in Jonkapath forest, when his son was three years old. Koka's widow remarried a co-villager after one year. She wanted to take her son with her to which her new husband also agreed. But Koka's grand-father did not allow the boy to go with his mother for fear of maltreatment.

Ronha of Rakaiya married Baryo of Durgapur. She came with two daughters, Kondi and Bahari. The former was deaf and dumb and the latter was a deaf and divorcee. Ronha arranged Kondi's marriage for which his wife looked for assistance from the son from her previous husband living in Durgapur. But she was refused financial assistance by his son who pleaded that after their mother's remarriage they were no longer responsible for her or her daughters because it was the duty of her new husband to take care of them. He however, attended his sister's marriage.

The ritual role of mother in the life cycle rites of her son is subsidiary in comparison to that of her husband but nevertheless important. In marriage of her son she plays an important role and her presence in most of the rituals is essential. She wears her best costumes on such occasions and decorates her body with ornaments and colourful cotton thread flowers.

When a Korwa woman becomes the grandmother of her son's children, her role becomes supervisory in the family and her relations with her son become more formal but not free from affection. She is never neglected by her son or son's wife and is looked after well till her death.

Father-Daughter

A female issue is considered as Lakshmi. A girl enhances the family income through the earning of bride-price. When the girl is young the father-daughter relationship is intimate. In his frequent sojourns outside the village the father keeps his daughter in his company whether he goes to the market or on a courtesy call to a kin living in other villages, or to attend a marriage or a fair. When she grows 3 to 4 years old, she is gifted by her father a miniature *dheki* (husking lever), a *supa* (winnowing fan) and several pieces of *garna* (food containers) as play-things. This intimacy fades out with the advancing age of the daughter. When she comes of age, the feeling of attachment with the father gives place to a sense of avoidance. She contributes her bit of responsibilities towards the collective socio-economic pursuits of her household by carrying out daily chores viz. taking goats for grazing, collecting roots, tubers, leaves and fruits from the forest, cleaning and sweeping of the house, cooking and washing clothes and attending to the younger siblings.

It is the responsibility of her father to get her a suitable husband. Although, a Korwa father has little financial responsibilities in the marriage of his daughter but if he fails in selecting a suitable husband for her and her marriage is broken she comes back to stay with him once more and again she has to be provided with a better spouse by her father. Father's home is the only place where a daughter can turn back for all kinds of help and assistance.

A father, unwilling to part with his daughter after marriage, seeks such a husband for her who may be agreeable to reside permanently with him as *gharjawain.* This may be taken as an evidence of the Korwa father's affection towards his daughter.

Mother-Daughter

Mother daughter relationship in the Korwa society is characterized by warmth, intimacy, co-operation, and a perfect mutual understanding. No sooner a Korwa girl attains the age of 5 or 6, she becomes an active helper to her mother in all socio-economic pursuits of the household. Her main responsibilities are to look after her younger siblings, helping her mother in various agricultural activities like thrashing and winnowing of food grains, cleaning utensils, fetching water, cleaning and sweeping the house, washing clothes, and fishing the mud.

The mother is considered by the Korwa society as the biggest loser in the marriage of her daughter. She loses not only a full-time associate and helper but also her best companion. The Hill Korwa are aware of this fact, thus, the mother's loss is made good by giving her the biggest share from the amount of bride-price (*mai-sari*).

When a daughter is married in another village, she is frequently visited by her mother. The daughter is a welcome guest in her mother's house. When a Korwa girl comes from her husband's house for the first time after her marriage, her mother takes her around the village and invites the villagers to see her daughter and son-in-law (*jawain*). When the daughter returns to her husband's house the mother sees her off at the village boundary. At the time of parting, the two burst into tears holding each other in a tight embrace.

In short, the relationship between mother and daughter is characterised by strong bond of affection, extreme cordiality, and a high degree of intimacy. This relationship receives a set back after the latter's marriage as there are fewer chances of meetings between the two but the inherent affection, intimacy, and cordiality in their relations never recede.

Brother-Brother

Relationship between two brothers in Korwa society is characterised by a sense of comradeship and mutual affection. Their association starts at an early age and lasts throughout their life. This prolonged association gets reinforced through their common experience of crises and calamities descending upon their household from time to time. They face all such situations unitedly.

Andhoo, Duggi, and Sukkhi of Rakaiya, lost their parents in early childhood. They were brought up by their maternal uncle. On coming of age, they could not stand the rude behaviour of their uncle and decided to settle at Rakaiya where they started working as *harwahas* (agricultural labourer) in the farm of Ashar Patel in a neighbouring village. Andhoo married Baloo's daughter, Duggi married Bajroo's daughter, and Sukkhi married Mahroo's daughter in the same village and were given tiny patches of land to build their houses by their respective fathers-in-law. When their maternal uncle died in Rakaiya the eldest brother participated in this burial ceremonies and failed to turn up to his master. The latter got very infuriated and gave heavy thrashings to his other brother Sukkhi till Sukkhi became unconscious. Gaining consciousness Sukkhi returned home with high fever resulting from injuries received from thrashings of the *grihat* (landlord). The next morning the youngest of the three brothers went to attend his work and experienced a similar treatment. Further, he was put under captivity, lest he should report the matter to the police. He was also threatened to face with dire consequence if he ever reported so. When Duggi failed to return home even late at night, his eldest brother got alarmed and walked to Shankargarh Police Station inspite of his high fever and body ache. After the police intervention that Sukkhan got Duggi released from the forced lock up by the *grihat*.

The brotherly feelings as reflected in the above narration is considered ideal. In the life situation they are not always free from friction and conflict.

Prabhu and Sukkhi of Maltipur were two brothers from the same mother but from different fathers. Sukkhi's son, Bodhna developed a fancy for Prabhu's daughter and brought her at his home against the wishes of his father Sukkhan and his eldest brother Prabhu. He performed *dhuku* marriage, which was found irregular by the *jat panchayat* and Bodhna's father Sukkhan was asked to pay Rs. 200/- as the bride-price to Prabhu which he paid. One year after marriage Budhna's wife died in pregnancy. Afterwards Sukkhan demanded from Prabhu a partial refund of the amount he had paid as bride-price on plea that inspite of paying a high amount of bride-price, the girl proved to be of no use for his son and his family. In case of his son's remarriage he will have to pay bride-price once more. Prabhu rejected Sukkhan's plea saying that the girl died due to the God's will. Sukkhan brought the matter before the *panchayat* but lost the case. This episode strained the relationship between the two brothers. Sukkhan complained bitterly about the alleged injustice done to him by his elder brother. The two severed all relations with one another.

Usually love and affection between two brothers not only last during their life time, but get reflected even after one of them dies. It is the responsibility of the living brother to look after the children of the deceased brother. It was found in all the four villages that atleast one family each was looking after the deceased elder brother's son/daughter.

Koka of Rakaiya was murdered in Jonkapath forest. His younger brothers Ratna and Nanka took an oath (*krya*) to take revenge. In June 1970, on the occasion of Kathori festival, Ratna took the alleged murderers to a nearby *bhatti* (distillery) and offered them liquor generously in order to make them weak to defend themselves. After making the alleged killers of his elder brother drink Ratna inflicted severe wounds of *balua* (axe) on them. Fortunately nobody died in the incident.

Relationship between the two brothers start as playmates and grows into intimacy with the passage of time. It is charactrised with regard for wishes of each other, obedience of elder brother by the younger, and considerate attitude of the elder brother towards his younger brother, irrespective of the fact whether they share the same roof of a house or live in different houses in the village or in different villages.

Sister-Sister

The elder sister to her younger brother sister is next only to the mother. Intimate relations between the two start from a very young age. The elder sister carries her younger siblings including younger sister but as the two girls grow old, their intimacy takes the form of a strong trust in each other. Sisters always move in a group. They go together in the forest for grazing cattle picking up cow-dung, and collecting forest products. Having known the mysteries of sex the two give enough latitude to one another keeping each other's secrets in strict confidence. Marriage of two sisters at different place brings a vital change in their mutual relationships. Having little chance of frequent meetings with each other the warmth of their relationship reduces.

Another dimension of sororal relationship among the Hill Korwa is in the form of the two sisters being co-wives of a common husband. In this situation they compromise and reconcile with their respective positions. Friction between sororal wives of a common husband is a rare phenomenon. They not only maintain their actual blood relations but honour each other's rights in a new situation they are put into. The elder sister acts as a senior wife and commands full respect from her younger sister. In return the elder sister co-operates with her younger sister in domestic chores. Their collective goal is to keep their common husband satisfied by their rightful conduct. This reconciliatory attitude of the two sisters is conditioned by their early relationship in which they learn to live as close companions and co-sharers of their mutual secrets.

Brother-Sister

In young age brother and sister behave as playmates, sleep together under the same roof, participate in *dumkach*, *karma* and *cherta* dances and take animals to the forest for grazing in each other's company.

The elder brother is responsible for the maintenance of his unmarried or divorced sister after the death of their father. In absence of father it is his responsibility to find out a suitable husband for his sister and solemnise the marriage.

Jugroo's elder sister in Rakaiya was married to Sukkhan of the same village some 30 years ago. Jugroo's father promised to present his son-in-law a bullock as a gift but he died without fulfilling his promise. Jugroo took the responsibility of making presentation to his sister's husband. After a lapse of 25 years, he presented the promised bullock to Sukkhan in presence of members of his and his sister's husband's clan. He declared that he was fulfilling his father's promise and apologised publicly that his poor financial condition was mainly responsible for the unusual delay in making presentation to his brother-in-law. All the guests were treated with food and tobacco was distributed among the members of Jugroo's clan who came from an adjoining village.

While going through household census cards it was found, 7 Korwa households were keeping their sister or sister's children. In two cases, the sisters were above 70 years of age and in 5 cases, either their husbands died or deserted. Subsequently they remarried leaving their children from their previous husbands under the custody of their brothers.

Grand-parents and Grand-children

The relationship between the two is warm, informal, and intimate in nature. When children are young they pass most of their time in the company of their grand parents. Young grand-children sleep with their grand parents in a separate hut (*koomba*). Before getting a round of sleep, the grandfather/mother rekindles fire inside the hut during winter and wraps children even with the only cover on his/her body. The children pass the evenings listening to the stories about the Maharaja and his chivalrous acts, about the old man's own skill as a hunter and his experiences with *chri* and *missan* (witches and ghosts).

Mahroo of Rakaiya was always seen with his three grand-children, Patro, two years, Chapli, six years and Bhola, eight years. Bhola was engaged with Nandi's daughter and Mehroo was anxious to get Bhola married during his own life time. He used to bring wild fruits from the forest. No sooner he would enter into the house, children would rush at him. On ceremonial occasions, he was seen offering *handi* (beer) to her grandchildren from his leaf cup.

A trace of joking is found in the grand-parent and grand-children relationship. Sometimes a grandmother addresses her grandson as her husband. The child blushes and in return teases his grandmother by his childish pranks.

Mother-in law Daughter-in-law

On completion of *biah* ceremonies when the bride is led towards her husband's house she cries bitterly but she is consoled by her kin. She is told by her elderly relatives that she is going to beget a new set of relatives in her husband's village: mother, father, grand-parents, uncles and aunts, brothers and sisters. This is an attempt to help the girl to face the new situations at case. As a matter of fact, a Korwa girl is trained from her early childhood to adjust herself in her husband's family. The gap between *mangabara* and *biah* helps the bride to adjust herself in her family of procreation. The attitude of a mother-in-law to a newly wedded daughter-in-law is of love and affection in case the girl is young, and mature girls are treated with sympathy, consideration, and co-operation by their mother-in-law. The mother-in-law helps making her son's wife understand the family tasks awaiting ahead. She watches the movements and activities of the newly initiated member of the family with utmost care.

If the bride belongs to the same village and has her father's house in proximity, there comes a sudden change in her behaviour towards her parents and siblings.

The house of Bajroo and Gudoo in Rakaiya were situated at a distance of about 100 metres. Bajroo's daughter, Pehti was married with Gudoo's son Jarha. Before her marriage Pehti used to come to the school building with her younger sibling for collection of CARE gifts. Soon after marriage it was observed that Pehti started coming with her husband's siblings and occasionally with her husband's father's younger brother, a blind old man of about sixty five of years age. She was ordinarily not seen in her father's house or with her own siblings any more. Instead she could be seen moving in the village in the company of her husband's mother and his younger siblings.

When Gudoo sent the proposal of his son's marriage with Pehti to Bajroo, the latter did not show his keenness giving an excuse of bad crop and his being deep in indebtedness. Gudoo's wife was in the advanced stage of pregnancy and she was unable to cook for her family consisting of eight members. Gudoo pressed the proposal further and Bajroo finally gave his consent. The marriage was performed hurriedly. No sooner Pehti reached in Gudoo's house, her mother-in-law gave birth to a child.

The nature of mutual inter-dependence between mother-in-law and daughter-in-law is, thus, functional. The two are badly in need of each other's help. If either of the two shirk away from her responsibility the harmony of their relationship is shattered. It will, however, be an erroneous assumption that their relationship is free from strains, frictions, and conflicts. A disloyal daughter-in-law and her waywardly behaviour pricks her mother-in-law resulting into conflicts and leading towards ultimate break of marriage between her son and daughter-in-law.

Sometimes a disloyal husband is stoutly defended by his mother who tries to see all defects in her daughter-in-law. This tendency creates a cleavage in otherwise harmonious relationship between the daughter-in-law and mother-in-law leading to final break of marriage. Thus, the relationship between the two is to a large extent dependent upon the nature of relationship between husband and wife.

REFERENCES

1. Mukherjee, Ramkirshna 1962. "On Classification of Family Structure" in *Indian Anthropology* Edited by T.N. Madan and Gopala Saran, New Delhi, Asia Publishing House: 352-398.

2. Murdock, G.P. 1960. *Social Structure*, New York, Macmillan: 223-224.

3. Karve, Iravati. 1953. *Kinship Organisation of India*, Poona. Deccan College: 284-289.

CHAPTER THREE

Economic Resources

Forest

The Hill Korwa, traditionally are forest dwellers. For them forest is their home, source of livelihood and part of life. It supplies their food and fuel. It is the abode of 'Mahadeo', the protector of the village, 'Satvahini', the goddess of wealth, 'Bughwait' and 'Shikari Dev' the deities responsible for providing plentiful forest products. Forest deities are implored for securing a bumper *mahua* crop.

The Hill Korwa, who lived in forests for hundreds of years enjoyed absolute freedom to exploit minor forest produces. They enjoyed privileges of utilising forest products as they liked till the middle of the nineteenth century when people from outside moved in the forest and started exploitation on commercial basis. Thus conditions began to change. The government introduced legislations in the national interest to protect forest from exploitation of the people. Policies were laid down to administer the forest areas for public benefit and to put restrictions on the privileges so far enjoyed by its inhabitants.

The policy was reassessed in 1952 by the Union Government because of the fact that the population of the country had increased by 40 per cent between 1894 and 1950 resulting into tremendous pressure on land and for securing forest and waste lands. The importance of forest for mitigating the climatic conditions in the economic field such as development of agriculture, industry, and communication was better understood. Taking the above facts into consideration a new policy was laid down by the Union Government in 1952. Thus forests owned by State or in private possession were re-classified as under ;

(a) Protected forests are those which have to be preserved or created for physical and climatic considerations.

(b) National forests are those to be maintained and managed to meet the needs of the defence, communication, industry and other general purpose of public importance.

(c) Village forests are to be maintained to provide timber for agricultural implements, local requirements and grazing and

(d) Tree lands are as which though outside the scope of the ordinary forest management are essential for the amelioration of the physical conditions of the country.

The implication of this new policy in context of the Hill Korwa, who, still lean heavily over the forest for satisfaction of their day-to day needs, was serious and affected their economy adversely.

Hunting still survives as a significant characteristic of their food-gathering economy. The forests, however, are largely devoid of games because of their intensive exploitation by the outsiders.

It is, thus, evident that the Hill Korwa had adopted forest as the main source of their livelihood. The material culture speaks of the flora of their surroundings, and their economy is mainly based on forest. Their aesthetic needs are attended to by forests which also fulfil their psychic needs. Hence, when the Hill Korwa ceased to be the bonafide users of the forest aud its products, their economy shattered. They felt numbed and lifeless with the desecration of the abode of their forest deities by the strangers. Guns of the forest contractors boomed day and night killing animals for fun. Now the forests of Surguja are devoid of Sambhar, Cheetal and Kotari which once abounded there. Killing of these once provided the Hill Korwa a sense of pride, fulsome food, and abundant fun. Now they feel deprived and dejected.

Food gathering and hunting supplements the Korwa food supply. Its main source is, however, the *beora* cultivation. With the increasing restrictions on exploitation of forest and its produces, the Hill Korwa were forced to stop the practice of *beora* cultivation, which reduced the tribe into a community of thieves and beggars.

Land

To an agricultural people land is the most important factor and labour, capital, and organisation are dependent on the amount of land available and on the nature of soil. The Hill Korwa being shifting cultivators in the recent past, treat land as a communal property. The idea of private ownership of land is yet to be perceived by the people.

After abolition of *beora*, the Hill Korwa were given forest tracts which they assiduously cleared and started settled agriculture. But the land given to the people was of extremely poor in quality and small in quantity,

TABLE 3.1

Land Types in Chhattisgarh

Type of land		Amount of rent per acre per annum (in Rs.)	Main crops
Bahra	I	3.00	Paddy sown by transplantation
Bahra	II	2.75	-do-
Chanwar	I	2.75	-do-
Chanwar	II	2.50	-do-
Bhatta	I	1.75	Paddy sown by transplantation or broadcasting.

Bhatta	II	1.50	Paddy sown by broadcasting only
Danr	I	0.50	Millets (Kodo, Madua, Gondli, Minjhry) Pulses (Urad, Moong, Kurthi) Oil seeds (Jantgi, Til)
Danr	II	0.31	Millets, lentils and oil seeds
Danr	III	0.19	Millets only
Bari		1.00	Mustard, Maize, Wheet, Gram, Urad, Moong and Vegetables.

The *bahra* land is low in situation and being close to the sources of irrigation is very fertile. The *bahra* paddy is sown in July and August, immediately after rains and is harvested in January. *Chanwar* and *bhatta* are inferior types of land in comparison to *bahra*, but paddy can be grown in them. Such lands are irrigated either by wells or rains. *Bari* land is attached with cultivator's household. *Danr* land is situated on hill slopes and is considered to be the most inferior in quality having no source of irrigation except rain water.

The Hill Korwa in all the four villages under study were found by and large in possession of mainly the *danr* land and small patches of *bari* land. The correct figures of ownership of land by its types could not be ascertained due to the non-availability of land records. But the Hill Korwa are mostly in possession of *danr* lands. Information collected from about 30 villages of Surguja and Raigarh Districts corroborate this fact.

The difficulty in collecting the accurate data on land is well-known. In three of the Hill Korwa villages the people were not in possession of revenue papers. Hence, figures on landholdings could not be collected from Bansajhal. Rakaiya being the forest village was transferred to Revenue Department at the time of investigation. Thus Revenue papers were not ready in Rakaiya. The people in Maltipur and Bansajhal also did not possess revenue papers. The number of land owning and landless households and their respective percentages have been produced for Rakaiya, Maltipur and Sardapath only as the revenue papers of Bansajhal were not available at the time of investigation. The number of landown ing landless households of the Hill Korwa given in the following table.

TABLE 3.2

Number of Landowning and Landless Korwa Households

	Rakaiya		Maltipur		Sardapath		Total	
		%		%		%		%
No. of landowning households	29	96.67	22	95.66	55	91.65	106	93.80
No. of landless households	1	3.33	1	4.34	5	8.35	7	6.20
Total	30	100.00	23	100.00	60	100.00	113	100.00

Out of 113 households, seven did not possess any land and 106 households owned landholdings varying between 0.61 acre (owned by Nadhia of Rakaiya) to 63.53 acres (Mira Ram of Sardapath) in size. Lands owned by the Hill Korwa of Surguja are smaller size in than those possessed by their brethren in Kaigarh.

The Table 3.3 shows the size of landholding possessed by the people in Rakaiya, Maltipur and Sardapath.

Table 12 shows that 85.00 per cent of Korwa households own landholdings upto 15 acres and only 15.00 per cent own landholdings above 15 acres. In Rakaiya, 44.82 per cent households own landholdings upto 5 acres only, while in Maltipur a fairly large number of households i.e., 36.38 per cent own landholdings between 5 and 10 acres. In Sardapath 67.28 per cent households own landholdings varying between 10 to 15 acres. Hence, the maximum size of landholdings possessed by the people falls below 15 acres.

In view of the poor quantity of land it can be said that land is not a substantial source of income for the people. The pattern of landowning in the three villages was found more or less uniform. In Rakaiya two households were cultivating land jointly. Budhwa of Rakaiya was cultivating the land of his deceased elder brother's son and Phauda was tilling the land of his grandson whose father was murdered sometime ago.

TABLE 3.3

Distribution of Households by Size of Landholdings

Amount of land owned (in acres)	VILLAGES Rakaiya	%	Malti-pur	%	Sarda-path	%	Total	%
0 - 5	13	44.82	6	27.26	-	-	19	17.92
5+ - 10	12	41.40	8	36.38	4	7.28	24	22.64
10+ - 15	3	10.34	7	31.81	37	67.28	47	44.34
15+ - 20	1	3.44	1	4.55	4	7.28	6	5.66
20+ - 30	-	-	-	-	5	9.09	5	4.72
30+ - 40	-	-	-	-	3	5.45	3	2.83
40+ -	-	-	-	-	2	3.62	2	1.89
Total	29	100.00	22	100.00	55	100.00	106	100.00

In Maltipur, Ghasi Ram and his father Sukkhan were cultivating their land jointly although Ghasi Ram was living separately and the land was not divided.

In Sardapath, 33 households were sharing land in 12 different land-pools which consisted of son's father, brother's-brother and the deceased brother's son both minor and major.

Table 13 shows the average size of landholdings possessed by a Hill Korwa household and an individual.

From the table it is seen that a Hill Korwa household owns a landholding of 10.82 acres with an average size of 5.71 members. On average, an individual owns 1.89 acres.

The average size of landholding at Sardapath is 14.47 acres. This is followed Maltipur having 10.17 acres on average. Rakaiya comes to the lowest in this respect having four acres of land per household of 4.8 members.

A similar picture emerges from the distribution of per capita landholding. A Hill Korwa at Sardapath, Maltipur, and Rakaiya owns 2.76, 1.30 and 0.83 acres of land respectively.

While camparing the Hill Korwa of two districts viz., Surguja and Raigarh, it was found that the Hill Korwa of Surguja lag far behind from those Raigarh in possession of landholdings.

The average household size of Hill Korwa of Surguja is 5.94 and average size of landholding per household is 7.58 acres. The average size of per capita landholding in Surguja is 1.27 acres. The average household size in Raigarh is 5.3 acres and the size of landholding per household 14.47 acres and per capita 2.76 acres. Hence, the Hill Korwa of Raigarh appear to have better control over land resources.

Some of Hill Korwa landowners are unable to cultivate their fields due to non-availability of input materials and draught animal. Hence they resort to the practice of share-cropping, which is locally known as *batai*. The rules of *batai* are as under :

1. The landowner gives his land to the party temporarily. The ownership of land remains unchanged.

TABLE 3.4

Size of Landholdings Per Household, Per Capita

Villages	No. of households	Total population	Average household size	Size of landholding per household (in acres)	Size of landholding per capita	Total amount of land (in acres)
Rakaiya	30	144	4.8	4.00	0.83	120.00
Maltipur	23	180	7.8	10.17	1.30	234.00
Sardapath	60	321	5.3	14.47	2.76	868.10
Total	113	645	5.71	10.82	1.89	1222.10

2. The owner is responsible for the safety and care of standing crops.
3. The share-croppers supply input materials and draught animals.
4. The yield including straw is divided equally between the landowner and the share-cropper.

Mortgage

A pressing need for cash money to meet eventualities like marriage of a family member, mourning in the family, or a punitive feast imposed by the panchayat drives an individual to mortgage his land with neighbouring tribes or non-tribal population. The custom of land mortgage is known as *bandha.* The owner of the land loses the right of exploitation of his land but remains its owner till such time as money is paid back in full. The person who takes land on mortgage pays to the mortgagee an agreed amount of money and is entitled to possess the yield from land till the money he gives to the mortgagee is returned in full. Such agreements are made verbally. Hence the Hill Korwa do not possess any written records about such dealings.

Labour

The following table shows the distribution of labour force.

TABLE 3.5

Percentage Distribution of Labour

Distribution	Rakaiya	Maltipur	Bansajhal	Sardapath
Auxiliary Labour	51.38	43.33	45.85	53.58
Regular Labour	48.62	56.33	54.15	46.42

For purpose of analysis the entire population under study has been divided into 4 age categories. These are from 0+ to 14, 15+ to 34, 35+ to 59 and 60 years and above. The first and the last categories constitute auxiliary labour force. It incorporates children upto 14 years and old adults above

60 years, of age. People between 15 years to 59 years of age constitute the category of regular labour. It has been observed that children upto 15 years and elderly persons above sixty years take responsibility of light jobs, nevertheless they take active part in economic chores of life. Hence, they have been put under auxiliary labour force. Individuals belonging to the age group of 15 to 60 years form the core of working force and and as such they have been put under regular force of the above table.

Children upto 6 years of age do not indulge in labour. From the age of 7 to 15 years they perform light jobs and supplement to the earning of regular labour force.

From the table it is evident that the Hill Korwa of Rakaiya and Sardapath have a higher proportion of auxiliary labour group and the people of Maltipur and Bansajhal have the higher percentage of regular labour. Sardapath has the maximum percentage of auxiliary labour force (53.58 per cent) which is closely followed by Rakaiya (51.38 percent). In regular labour Maltipur has the highest percentage (56.67 per cent) which is followed by Bansajhal (54.15 per cent).

The modes of self employment, which will be dealt at length in the next chapter, can be briefly put as hunting, food gathering, fishing, construction of house, and agricultural and household activities. Besides, employment of various nature like digging of soil, agricultural labour, porterage etc., are done for members of other groups in order to earn cash money and supplement their income.

As the job opportunities are very few in the area, the Hill Korwa usually resort to agricultural labour. Communities that employ the people are the Mahto (Ahir), Kawar, Bihari Muslims, Nagesia, and Oraon.

Korwa men and women actively participate in economic activities of their households which is the basic unit of labour. Children do not lag behind their elders and take active part in economic pursuits of their respective households. Though there is some amount of over-lap between a man's and a woman's job, division of labour on the basis of sex and age has been observed. The following table illustrates division of labour in economic pursuits between men, women, and children.

TABLE 3.6
Division of Labour

Men	Women	Children
Ploughing, sowing, digging of earth, manufacture, of bows, arrows, ploughs and fire making by simple drill.	Carrying loads, earth, supplying building material for construction of house.	Catching birds, fowls, tending cattle, fishing in shallow water.
Collection of palm leaves and its processing for manufacture of palm mats.	Plaiting of mats, barter and sale of agricultural produces making of leaf cups and plates.	Collecting mahua flowers, helping parents in agricultural activities.
Digging tubers by a dibble	Processing of tubers	
Reaping threshing, ploughing, harrowing, watching standing crops.	Collection of fuels, cooking, drying and watching of mahua flowers, washing of clothes and utensils, sweeping and cleaning house.	—
Cooking (only in emergency) working in farms as agricultural labourers, processing, filtering and distributing beer of mahua and millets.	Poultry raising and raising kitchen gardens.	Taking cattle and goats to the forest for grazing.

It appears that there is no rigid division of labour based on sex in the society. Women, however are not allowed to touch a plough (*hardeo*) which symbolises a deity lest they should invite the risk of its fury. Many of the men's job are also done by women, while men relax. During menstruation and pregnancy a woman is forbidden to cook and in absence of any other female member in the household a man cooks for himself and the children.

Marketing once a week is a common engagement of both men and women. In market, most of the purchasing is done by women while men pay for the purchased commodities. Similarly, child rearing activities are shared equally by the two. During infancy, the major burden of bringing up a child falls on the mother's shoulders but as the time passes, a child is looked after equally by both the parents.

Midwifery is the specialised job of the aged Korwa women. In Rakaiya a woman of 80 years who left the occupation recently due to her failing eyesight helped in delivery of twelve children. Most of them are now married. Before retiring from her occupation the old woman trained four women of the village in her profession who now cater to the need of the villagers.

The hardest phase of life requiring maximum labour out put for eking out a livelihood starts from the late teens. Being married, by this age the boys maintain their separate family, if the parents are unable to accommodate them in their own house while the girls after marriage share their husband's heavy responsibilities. Some respite from this hard labour, however, comes with the children attaining adolescence. Couples having no male issue, carry the burden of hard labour till their death. If the overall economic condition of a Korwa household is sound, the father prefers to keep his daughter and her husband in his own household as *ghārjawain.* But such a respite from labour also proves to be of short lived as no sooner the daughter begets an issue, she has little time to share the burden of her parents. A Korwa couple having male issue is free from strenuous labour no sooner their sons come of age and help them in various occupations. After the sons marriage, parents get additional labour force in the form of newly inducted brides in the household.

Persons of 60 years and above do not participate in hard manual labour. They assume a supervisory role. A man in the above age group if strong in physique, indulges in self-employed labour. He, however, does not accept employment elsewhere. His job is to supervise his household affairs and settle disputes within and with other households of the village. He negotiates marriage terms and represents his household on all community issues.

The agricultural labourers (*harwaha*) work in the farm of local petty landlords (*grihat*) in order to supplement family earnings for 6 or 7 months in a year. Both landowning and landless Korwas resort to labour with the *grihat*. The following table furnishes an overall situation of farm labour.

TABLE 3.7

Percentage of Agriculture Labourers

Villages	Total population	No. of Harwahas	Percentage
Rakaiya	144	10	6.94
Maltipur	180	8	4.44
Bansajhal	205	15	7.31
Sardapath	321	30	9.34
Total	850	63	7.47

The above table shows that 7.47 per cent of the Korwa population earns their living through agricultural labour. The percentage of *harwahas* is the highest in Sardapath (9.34) and then in Bansajhal (7.31). Rakaiya comes next with 6.94 per cent and Maltipur is characterised by the lowest percentage of farm labourers having 4.44 per cent.

Agricultural labourers are locally known as *harwahas*. There are two types of labourers: (i) casual labourers, and (ii) contract labourers. The casual labourers are paid daily wages in kind, i.e., 3 seers of millets per day. Contract labouıers are appointed for a term of one year from the month of *Aghan* (October-November) on a payment of Rs. 66 per annum in addition to 18 maunds of food grains consisting of millets, maize, and paddy. The type of grain given in the form of remuneration to a *harwaha* depends on the convenience of his master (*grihat*). In Rakaiya, it was reported that in the first four months of the year maize, for the next five months millets and in the remaining three months paddy is given as a part of wages.

The working hours for a *harwaha* start from the dawn to the late night. At hour's respite, however, is given in the afternoon enabling labourers to prepare their meals. They are also granted one day's leave after every 9 working days enabling them to look after their own agricultural operation. It is more a convention rather than a rule which is observed by very few *grihats*. The *harwahas* in Rakaiya complained that they were forced to work throughout the year without any leave privileges. Prolonged working hours force *harwahas* to construct temporary shelters near the place of work in case it is not possible for them to go to their respective village in the late hours of the night and return early in the next morning.

It was observed that in Rakaiya and Bansajhal, the population of agricultural labourers practice farm labour as the primary source of livelihood due to non-availability or poor quality of land but in Maltipur and Sardapath, they work in order to supplement their income. Hence, for them labour is the secondary source of livelihood.

The participation of Hill Korwa in white-collar jobs is non-existent with a lone exception of a matriculate Hill Korwa of Sardapath working as a Primary School Teacher in a neighbouring village

In Surguja, the Korwa Red Turban Chiefs get a remuneration of Rs. 12/- per mensem, a red turban and a shirt per annum. There are 13 red Turban Chiefs in Surguja District but none hails from the villages under study.

The Korwa Patels get commission on the revenue they collect from the villagers. Chadra Patel of Maltipur was the only Korwa Patel in the four villages under study, who was getting Rs. 36/- per annum as his commission for the amount he collected as land revenue for his co-villagers.

The duties performed by a *harwas* are manifold and the nature of duty depends on the sweet will of the *grihat*. To enumerate a few; maintenance of irrigation channels, ploughing, weeding, harvesting, threshing, winnowing, and making stores of fuel wood for the *grihat*. They are responsible for taking herds for grazing and protecting the standing crops against dangers of stray animals, thieves and fire. They are also engaged in building up the *kharyan* (granary) and construction and repairs of the *grihat* house.

Capital

Besides land and labour, capital is also an important economic resource. Capital represents, "a stock of goods and services not devoted to immediate consumption but operated to increase the volume of consumption in future periods, either directly or indirectly through production."

The investments made by the Hill Korwa for the purpose of capital formation are very few and can be counted on finger tips. Ornaments made of alloy which are used by the majority of people have little value in terms of money but new some women invest in silver ornaments. Mahuari of Rakaiya, a widow care-taker of her landowning son possessed silver ornaments worth Rs. 50/- from the produces of her son's land. She also invested a part of her savings (Rs. 40/-) in taking Sanya's land on mortgage for a period of one year. Sanya could not return the money within the stipulated time and failed to get back his land from Mahuari.

Other forms of capital are livestock and poultry. Bullocks are used in agricultural operations. Goats and pigs are raised for use during ceremonial occasions like marriage. Poultry is mainly raised for the deities to whom they are sacrificed from time to time in order to receive a bumper crop, ample forest produces and freedom from illness. Cows are kept for procreating oxen and also as milching animals. They use milk for preparing small quantities of *ghee* for self consumption. The following table gives a comprehensive picture of the cattle wealth possessed by the Hill Korwa of the four village under study:

TABLE 3.8

Distribution of Cattle Owning and Non-Cattle Owning Households

Villages	No. of households	No. of cattle owning households	Percentage	No. of households without cattle	Percentage
Rakaiya	30	19	63.33	11	36.67
Maltipur	23	16	69.57	7	30.43
Bansajhal	36	19	52.78	17	47.22
Sardapath	60	43	71.67	17	28.33
Total	149	97	65.10	52	34.90

According to the above table 65.10 per cent of the Hill Korwa households own animal wealth cousisting of bullock, buffaloes, cows and goats and 34.90 per cent do not possess any animal wealth. Sardapath tops in possession of animal wealth as 71.67 per cent households of the village own animals. Maltipur comes next with 69.57 per cent. Nearly 63 per cent household at Rakaiya own animal wealth. Bansajhal comes at the bottom with only 52.78 per cent of its Korwa households owning animals.

After having a look at the animal wealth in possession of the Hill Korwa, it is necessary to show the number of animals possessed per household and per capita.

Table 18 shows that a Korwa household possesses 2.17 animals: 1.46 bullocks, 0.72 goats. Looking at the distribution by village and of animal wealth per household, it can be observed that like other economic resources Sardapath tops in animal wealth also. A household possesses 1.83 bullocks, 0.57 cows and 1.18 goats. Thus, a household in Sardapath owns 3.58 animals, roughly three times of Rakaiya and double of Bansajhal. Next to Sardapath comes Maltipur where a house-

TABLE 3.9

Animal Wealth

Villages	No. of House-holds	Population	Number of animals				Number of animals per household				Number of animals per capita			
			Bullocks	Cows	Goats	Total	Bullocks	Cows	Goats	To'al	Bullocks	Cows	Goats	Total
Rakaiya	30	144	22	1	14	37	0.73	0.03	0.47	1.23	0.15	0.01	0.10	0.26
Maltipur	23	175	46	5	16	67	2.00	0.22	0.69	2.91	0.26	0.03	0.09	0.38
Bansajhal	36	201	39	4	7	50	1.08	0.11	0.19	1.38	0.19	0.02	0.04	0.25
Sardapath	60	321	110	34	71	215	1.83	0.57	1.18	3.58	0.34	0.11	0.22	0.67
Total	149	841	217	44	108	369	1.46	0.29	0.72	2.17	0.26	0.05	0.13	0.44

hold possesses 2.91 animals: 2.00 bullocks, 0.22 cows and 0.69 goats. A household in Bansajhal possesses 1.38 animals: 1.08 bullocks, 0.11 cow and 0.19 goat. Rakaiya occupies the lowest place with 1.23 animals possessed by a household: 0.73 bullocks: 0.03 cow and 0.47 goat.

A Korwa individual in the four villages of Chattisgarh possesses 0.44 animal: 0.26 bullock, 0.05 cow and 0.13 goat. The per capita distribution of animal wealth is the highest in Sardapath where an individual owns 0.67 animal: 0.34 bullock, 0.11 cow, and 0.22 goat. Next comes Maltipur where an individual possesses 0.38 animal: 0.26 bullock, 0.03 cow and 0.09 goat. In Bansajhal an individual possesses 0.25 animal: 0.19 bullock, 0.02 cow and 0.04 goat. Rakaiya shows the minimum quantity of animals owned by an individual which stands at 0.26 animal: 0.15 bullock, 0.01 cow and 0.10 goat.

The author has excluded poultry as he found that poultry birds are not raised with any economic motive. If someone approaches a Hill Korwa for buying chicken, the latter refuses to part with on the pretext of their being dedicated to deities. A chicken is sacrificed in almost all socio-religious rituals whether observed individually or collectively and then consumed by the people. Thus, poultry does not help the Hill Korwa in the process of capital formation. Poultry indirectly helps in enhancing the Korwa capital as a chicken is sacrificed to a particular deity for a bumper output of food grains, abundant mahua crop, a safe journey through the forest, and good health. Absence of such propitiation may adversely affect the process of capital formation.

Table 3.10 shows a comparative picture of economic resources under control of the Korwa of the four villages under study.

Land

Rakaiya is deficient in land resources. Although, the percentage of landless households is only 3.33 but 44.82 per cent of the landowning households own less than 5 acres and 86.22 per cent own less than 10 acres. As mentioned earlier, there are no arrangements for irrigation and the quality of land

TABLE 3.10

Economic Resources

Villages	No. of households	Average household size	Average size of household land-holding (in acres)	Per capita size of land-holding (in acres)	Percentage of landless households	Percentage of bullock owning households	Percentage of cow owning households	Percentage of goat owning households	Percentage of agricultural labourers (Harwahas)
Sardapath	60	5.3	14.47	2.76	8.33	56.67	30.00	55.00	9.34
Maltipur	23	8.9	10.17	1.30	4.34	09.57	17.39	11.74	4.44
Bansajhal	36	5.5	N.A.*	N.A.*	N.A.*	47.22	27.78	11.11	7.31
Rakaiya	30	4.8	4.00	0.83	3.33	46.67	3.33	13.33	6.94

*Data not available.

owned by the Korwa is very inferrior. It is observed that 3.33 per cent households are landless and 9.34 per cent work as agricultural labourers. Hence, it is evident that atleast 3.61 per cent households are engaged simultaneously in cultivation as well as labour activities besides hunting and food gathering in order to supplement their income. The average size of landholding possessed by a household of 4.8 members is 4 acres. Hence an individual in Rakaiya possesses only 0.83 acre of land.

Among the three villages from where land records could be obtained Rakaiya occupies the lowest place in the size of landholding possessed by a household as well as an individual. The corresponding figures from Maltipur and Sardapath per household are 10.17 acres and 14.47 acres and per capita are 1.30 acres and 2.76 acres respectively. Dependence on agricultural labour by landowning households is minimum in Maltipur where only 0.10 per cent households depends simultaneously on agriculture and wage labour. In Sardapath 1.01 per cent households depend both on agriculture and wage labour for eking out their livelihood.

Sardapath shows the highest percentage of landless households (8.33 per cent) but bigger size of household landholdings and per capita possession of land lessens the severity of the problem of landlessness. The table shows that 7.31 per cent household in Bansajhal are landless, although figures about the size of landholdings possessed by a household and an individual are not available from the village but by observation it can be said that the amount of land available to the people is not sufficient to meet their food requirement.

Cows

Only one household in Rakaiya owns a cow. About 17 per cent households in Maltipur own cows the number of which per household varies between one and two. Bansajhal is better off in this respect where 27.78 per cent of households own cows. The number of cows owned by households varies between one to four. Sardapath comes at the top as 30.00 per cent of its households own cows, the number of which varies between one and seven.

Goats

Only 11.11 per cent households from Bansajhal own goats and the number of which per household varies between 1 and 3. Rakaiya is slightly better off than Bansajhal in this respect. Here 13.33 per cent households own goats the number of which varies between 1 to 9. In Maltipur 21.74 per cent households own goats and number of goats possessed per household varies between 2 to 4. Sardapath comes on the top in this respect. Fifty five per cent of the families own goats the number of which per household varies between 1 and 8.

Insignificant animal wealth is one of the indicators of poor rural economy. With 1.46 bullocks in average per household it is not possible for a Hill Korwa household to carry out agricultural operations independently. Therefore, either they resort to hire a bullock at a exhorbitant rate of 10 maunds of paddy/millet per head of cattle or to share-cropping which sometimes leads to mortgage or in most of the cases alienation of land.

The reason for low occurrence of cows among the Korwa may be attributed to the fact that people prefer to buy bullocks for agricultural operations. Goats are more in number than cows as the same are required to be slaughtered during marriages or mourning feasts. Only the privileged Korwa like Banya of Bansajhal keep cows following the footsteps of their immediate Mahto neighbourers. Thus keeping cows enhances social prestige. The Hill Korwa neither relish milk nor milk products but keep the animals with a view to perform agricultural operations and consume its flesh whenever any occasion arises. Cows are exceptions but they produce not only male calves but fetch a good price for itself and the by-products. Extraction of manure is a by-product of animals.

Taking animal wealth as a whole into account, we find that Sardapath is on the top and Rakaiya is at the bottom. Maltipur comes nearer to Sardapath whereas Bansajhal is close to Rakaiya.

REFERENCES

1. Firth, Raymond. 1969. "Capital, Saving and Credit in Peasant Societies—A viewpoint from Economic Anthropology" in *Capital, Saving and Credit in Peasant Societies,* Edited by Raymond Firth and B.S. Yamey, London George Allen and Uniwin : 18.

CHAPTER FOUR

Economic Activities

The relationship between man and his immediate environment or habitat gives rise to the concept of ecology which has been defined as "the science of inter-relation beween living organisms and their environment".[1] It is an erroneous presumption that "savage" is a "man who, commonly living in a climate where his needs are bountifully provided by nature neither is required to exert himself nor is willing to do so when he can obtain even the necessary minimum to support life by abstaining from effort."[2]

A charge of laziness is levied against the Hill Korwa too, whose apathy towards the settled agriculture and other schemes of planned development are cited by the agents of change as an example. A Hill Korwa does as much work as he feels it is sufficient to fulfil his basic demands of getting a living from nature.

Food gathering

The Hill Korwa, as stated earlier were the shifting cultivators in the past and even now they depend heavily on forest for eking out their livelihood. The forest produces which are collected by them people may be put into two categories. The first consists of non-edible produces and the second edible. Non-edible forest produces collected by the people are fuel wood, timber, bark, and leaves. The edible produces are, various kinds of fruits, tubers, twigs, flowers, roots, leaves and games.

Non-edible forest produces

Collection of fuel wood is done during nine months a year. Fuel wood is essential for consumption and also supplement their income during lean months of rainy season. Timber is extracted for house construction and repairs and also for erection of *madua* at the time of marriage.

A Korwa goes in the forest for collection of fuel along with other members of his household. The male members fell a tree and children start cutting its branches with their small axes while the female members collect branches and put them together in order to carry them easily as *bhar*. Each load of wood is about 40 kgs. in weight and two loads of wood are tied on the two ends of a five feet long sturdy poll which is balanced on shoulders and transported. Adult female members of the household put a heavy log of wood on their head and children make a light load of small branches for carrying wood home on their heads. The loads brought from the forest are piled in a corner of open courtyard allowing wood to dry.

Fuel wood stocks are built from October to June. The maximum consumption of fuel wood is required during winters when the people observe marriage ceremonies. It is the time when the harvest is over and people enjoy their leisure time. As described earlier, the Hill Korwa are scantily dressed and have little protection against the biting cold of winter nights. Hence each household is required to burn wood to keep the huts warm. After taking *biyari* (night meals) the people kindle fire and go to sleep. The fire extinguishes in the midnight. The people wake up and rekindle the fire in order to get sufficient warmth till the break of dawn.

During rainy season, the Hill Korwa are unable to procure forest products. By this time, the food grains are completely exhausted so also most of the wild fruits like *tendu, mahua* mango, *piyar* and jack fruit. The only source of livelihood at that time is by selling fire wood which fetches them a meal or two in a day. A load of 80 kgs of wood fetches an individual half a rupee or three *pallas* of paddy/millets.

Timber is mainly required for building houses or erecting *mandua* for performance of marriage ceremonies. The Hill Korwa are allowed to remove timber from the unrestricted forests on paying animal change to the State Forest Department.

Bark is extracted for making ropes and pouches (*potil*). The latter is used as a container which is kept and pressed between the two overlying planks of an oil crusher (*patni*). A few Hill Korwa sell these for a quarter of a rupee each to their neighbours.

Leaves which are collected from the forest are of *sarai* (Shorea robusta), *palas* (Butea frondosa) and toddy palm. *Sarai* leaves are collected for making receptacles for serving food and drinks, known as *dona* and *phani* respectively or for making small conical leaf huts (*koomba*). *Palas* leaves are also collected for the same purposes. Toddy palm leaves are collected from the forest and are allowed to dry in the sun. The dried leaves are then put in water for making them tender. Narrow strips from palm leaves are made and a number of finished strips are stitched by bark to make a mat of 4′ x 6′ which is used by the people as a substitute for bed. Bamboo is used for making bows only.

Edible forest products

The most important edible forest product for the Hill Korwa are flowers of *mahua* (Bassia latifolia). From April to the middle of June, the Korwa village present a deserted look as a major part of villages population goes out to the forest for collecting *mahua* flowers. Before the flowering season of *mahua* new baskets are purchased and old ones repaired. Each member of the household goes to the forest holding a basket in hand. The collection of *mahua* flowers is done from early morning till noon. Sometimes a leaf shade is made right under the tree in order to facilitate the collection of flower. Fresh *mahua* flowers which taste sweet are eaten. Stale flowers are eaten boiled. The flowers are spread on a clean surface in the open and are allowed to get dry for three or four days. The dry flowers are stored in large containers made of *mohlain* leaves for future consumption or sale. The lady of the house pounds dried flowers into a thick paste on a mortar by help of a wooden pestle. It is then mixed with millet flour and cakes are prepared. *Mahua* flowers provide a fine substitute for jaggery to the Hill Korwa. These flowers are also used for preparing *jagra* beer. Dry *mahua* flowers are sold to co-operative societies at the rate of Rs. 9 per maund. It was observed that every family in Rakaiya sold 2 to 3 maunds of *mahua* flowers to the co-operative society at Shankargarh. By the middle of May, *mahua* fruits supplement Korwa diet. Thus *mahua* trees, flowers, fruits provide a relief to Hill Korwa in their food problem from middle of March to the middle of May and also bring them some cash income which is vital to meet their essential needs.

Amba (mango) is a favourite summer fruit. Korwa women and children go to the forest and collect baskets full of raw mangoes. The fruit is consumed raw but sometimes its kernel is ground with salt and chillies to make delicious *chatni* which is eaten with millet cakes or rice. Small amount of ripe mangoes are collected from the middle of May to the end of June and eaten.

Another important item which abounds the forests is jack fruit (*kathal*). A full grown ripe fruit weighs about seven kgs. The raw fruit is picked up from the forest, cut into pieces and eaten after boiling with chillies and salt. The ripe fruit is relished highly by the people. A single fruit is sufficient for an average Korwa household for a day. Its seeds are also boiled or fried in oil with spices. It makes a delicacy to the Korwa. Jack fruit is collected from middle of April till the end of June.

Doomar or *gular* fruits are also available in plenty. The popularity of the fruit can be assessed from the fact that many a Korwa settlement are named after it e.g., like Doomar-path, Doomar-para or Doomar-gaon. *Doomar* fruits are picked up in the months of May and June. The ripe fruit is eaten raw. Neither it is dried nor processed. *Bel*, *khirni lhasora* and *amli* (tamarind) are collected beween April and June.

Other fruits which are collected from middle of May till the end of July are : *piyar, jamun* and *ber*.

Honey is called *ras* and is found in deep forests. It is consumed by the people themselves. It is procured in little quantities and sold to the local *grihats* at the rate of Rs. 8/-per kg. The method of honey collection is by fumigating the hive. A man then climbs on the tree and plucks the beehive and puts it in a container. The beehive is then crushed by hands and the juice is collected in a leafy cup. The residue is eaten raw by all young and old.

Once, this author was going with a group of six Hill Korwa amidst dense forests of Jonkapath. Suddenly two of them ran towards a not-too-bulky tree and started blowing its trunk with axe. Soon the remaining persons joined the venture and grounded the tree within minutes. One of them put his hand inside the hollow trunk and picked out a fresh beehive with juice still dripping from it. A leafy cup was instantaneously made, the hive was put inside and the container was wrapped in a cloth. When asked how could they know about the beehive inside the hollow trunk, one of the two who gave first blows to the tree replied that he saw a bee going inside the trunk. By this, he concluded that a bee will enter only in a hollow trunk containing the beehive.

Young shoots of bamboo, tamarind, *churai*, *peepar kachnar bar* are collected by women and children from the forest. The leaves are boiled with salt and chillies and eaten with maize and millet cakes.

Among the tubers, *pitharoo kanda* which is rarely found is supposed to be the best in taste and is eaten raw. Other tubers collected from forests are *saidoo kandu,osair kanda, gainth kanda, doodhia kanda, nawka kanda* and *bajra kanda. Gainth kanda* is very bitter in taste hence the method of its processing is more elaborate than those of other tubers.

Digging tubers start with the onset of spring by a dibble (*khanti*). Tubers can be recognised by examining leaves. One can see hundreds of pits dug in the deep forest as a mark of digging tubers.

Members of a household go early in the morning in search of tubers with small bamboo baskets. The head of the household holds the dibble. Women and children scan forest in search of tuber-bearing plants. The head of the household in the meantime digs land at several spots to see if there are tubers hidden in the ground as sometimes leaves wither away due to heat. Whosoever spots the tuber calls other members of the household. Men dig the earth and women extract the tuber, clean it of dust, and put into baskets. Other tribes and castes of the area who do not consume tubers ascribe root-digging only to the Hill Korwa. Thus, tubers have no value in the local markets and the entire quantity is consumed by the collectors.

Hunting

Hunting is the significant feature of food gathering activities of the Hill Korwa. It is purely a masculine job. The Korwa skill of aiming and shooting an animal by a bow and arrow has won them appreciation from the local people and the rulers of the area. The Maharaja of Surguja, Ramanujasharan Singh Deo used to go for hunting invariably with a group of Hill Korwa. Many old Hill Korwa around Rakaiya and Jonkapath claim to have accompanied the Maharaja on his hunting expeditions. Birjhoo, the ex-Lotadar of Biria and Theppa Ram of Laldara (Surguja) were among many others who narrated their experiences of the hunting expedition in the company of the Maha raja.

Preparations for hunting expedition begin from April. New arrow-heads and iron blades for axes are purchased from the local iron smiths and the old ones are repaired. The iron parts of the hunting implements are sharpened by rubbing them against stone.

Twenty to thirty persons participate in a hunting expedition. All members of the team cover front portion of their body below the abdomen with green *sarai* leaves. This is done in order to deceive animals. As soon as the hunters enter into the forest equipped with bows and arrows, a few membersof the team take position behind big boulders. Others make a bee-line in front of boulders where hunters have taken position. The line slowly becomes a crescent and then a circle. All those included in the circle shout hoarsely and beat tin cans in order to frighten animals. The frightened animals run helter-skelter and the hunters sitting behind boulders shoot them with arrows.

The kill is brought to the village and all participants get equal share. Dogs accompanying the team also receive equal share.

Once during the investigator's stay in the area ten villagers in Rakaiya killed a hare weighing about 500 gms. The meat was divided into ten equal shares and was put into ten leaf cups. Each participant received one leafy container.

When a *cheetal* or *sambhar* is killed, the meat is bartered in the local market for an equal amount of rice. During the author's stay in Korwa villages no such transaction took place.

Hunting expeditions are organised on intra as well inter-village basis. Inter-village hunting expeditions have an advantage of covering a bigger area of forest and hence a higher chance of getting games. The method of distribution of game is the same as that of intra-village hunting expeditions.

Trapping

Trapping of animals and birds is not popular among the Hill Korwa, who, as expert archers, look down upon the practice. Only boys of 7 or 8 years keep a gum-trap (*lassa*) for trapping birds.

Another kind of trap usually used by the Hill Korwa of Maltipur and Sardapah is *kheencha phanda*. This trap has perhpas been acquired by the Hill Korwa from their neighbouring Oraons.

Fishing

Fishing is not a regular or substantial means of livelihood for the Hill Korwa. Most of the Hill Korwa villages are situated on hill tops or slopes. Therefore, tanks are not found around the Korwa settlements. The rivers and streams go dry between the middle of April to the middle of May. This is the time when the Korwa children participate in fishing activities. Fishing is also performed in the month of Kuar (September-October).

Three methods of fishing are prevalent among the people. The methods are: (a) by traps, (b) by bunding and (c) by poisoning water.

A trap is pitched in muddy water and fish is picked out from the trap with hands. In bunding, a portion of stream is blocked and water is drained out. Fishes are captured by hands.

Two ingredients are used for poisoning water. In Kartik, water is poisoned by the powder of *mauna* fruit and in Jeth it is done by the powder of *granj* roots. The powder is sprinkled on the surface of water and is thoroughly mixed by hands and feet. After sometime fish get stupefied and float on the surface of water and are picked up by the people.

Fishing is done by households independently, and unlike the hunting products it is usually consumed by members of the household.

The people remain occupied with food gathering activities throughout the year excepting the three rainy months of Asadh, Sawan, and Bhado, when movement becomes difficult due to rains, causing spate in rivers and streams. An additional danger involved in food gathering during these months is fear of poisonous insects and snakes which swarm the area. The rainy season is the most difficult period for the Hill Korwa whose stocks of food grains are almost exhausted and food gathering activities come to a halt due to heavy rains. The first millet crop comes not before the middle of September and the people have little opportunity to get a job with the local *grihats* who feel reluctant to employ casual Korwa labourers, but are more generous in extending loans to the starving Korwas. The only source of livelihood left to the people is to supply fuelwood, which is in great demand among the neighbouring people during rains. The supply of wood also becomes problem due to difficult road conditions. Bajroo of Rakaiya, thus, described the ordeals of the rainy season in the following words.

TABLE 4.1

Food Gathering Schedule

Local name of months	English equivalent	Non-agricultural activities
Magh	January-February	Collection of leaves, tubers, fuel wood.
Phagun	February-March	-do-
Chait	March-April	Collection of *mahua* flowers, leaves, fuel wood, timber, raw tamarind and mango fruits. Repair of hunting implements.
Baisakh	April-May	Digging of tubers, gathering of *mahua* flowers, fuel wood and leaves both edible and non-edible. Collection of fruits.
Jeth	May-June	Collection of mango, tamarind, raw jack furit, digging of tubers. hunting and fishing, drying and processing of *mahua* flowers.
Asadh	June-July	Fuel wood collection.
Sawan	July-August	Little gathering activities due to rains.
Bhadon	August-September	-do-
Kuar	September-October	-do-
Kartik	October-November	Fishing by poisoning water. Collection of fuel wood and leaves.
Aghan	November-December	Collection of leaves, fuel wood and timber for building the house and agricultural implements.
Pous	December-January	-do-

"If one survives in *barkha* (rainy season) one can hope to survive throughout the year',.

Animal husbandry

The tribals of Chattisgarh have *batai* system in which animals are given by their owner to the custody of a person on yearly basis. The custodian gets a half of the milk products and off-spring from the owner of the animal. This system is common especially in case of goats. The number of goats given to the custodian is taken back intact but milk and kids are divided into two equal shares, a half of which goes to the owner and another half to the custodian who is responsible for grazing and general upkeep of animals. The system has the initial advantage of providing milk and animals to those who do not possess any and the actual owner, on the other hand, is relieved from the responsibility of grazing his animals.

Ghurti of Rakaiya kept five goats of her neighbour Kondi for three years. The herd grew to 9 heads of goats and seven kids. In the meantime Kondi got married and wanted to get back her goats. Ghurti readily agreed to return seven goats and three kids and she got herself two goats and three kids. When the herd was led to Kondi's house Ghurti cried for hours lamenting that her house had become deserted. Her husband, three sons and eldest son's wife were seen consoling her.

Ghildren upto the age of 8 or 9 years take goats for grazing to the forest at the dawn and return at noon to have the mid-day meal (*kelwa*). They again take the herd to the forest and return after sunset. Bells made of wood or metal are tied around the neck of all animals. The bell helps the keeper of the herd to trace animals in thickness of forest by the sound of the bell.

No sooner a herd returns home, the head of the household counts their number. If he finds any animal missing he goes to the forest to bring it back.

The Hill Korwa have evolved a corporate system for grazing cows and bullocks. Young boys assume the responsibility of grazing animals belonging to various households of the village on yearly contract. The contract starts from the month of

Aghan (November-December) every year. On the occasion of Amass, the Hill Korwa perform Lakmi Puja (cow worship) and the custodian of the herd is given a quarter of a rupee in cash by each cattle owning househeld.

The rate of remuneration for grazing of goats paid by the owners to the grazer of the herd is 10 kgs of food grain per head of cattle per year.

In Rakaiya three boys, Padua (14 years), Sohra (12 years), and Baja (9 years) took contract for grazing village animals. Padua earned six maunds of millets by grazing animals in the preceding year. The next year all the six households the animals of which were in his custody retained him as the caretaker of their cattle. Seeing the earnings of Padua, Soha ra and Baja also took the contract for the first time. Batai system and collective grazing of animals are confined among members of the tribe only. Other tribes of the area do not give their cattle to the Hill Korwa because of the suspicion that the latter would poison the animals and eat the carrion.

When a bullock or cow dies, its skin is removed by the Chamar after paying a fee of Rs. 3. Goat's skin is removed by the Ghasia free of cost. The Ghasia are professional dancers and drummers and are supposed to perform dancing for the family concerned on special occasions like *mangabara* and *biah*. They utilise the goat's skin for making drums.

Cow-dung is collected by the children assiduously and dumped in a pit situated at the backyard of a cattle shed. The Hill Korwa use cow-dung exclusively for manuring their fields and plastering walls and floor of the house.

Horticulture

The Hill Korwa planted many a fuirt trees in their former *beora* fields which are now declared as Reserved Forests. They never cut any tree the fruits of which are eaten by them. Some informants told the author that such tree as planted by their ancestors are still in existence in the Reserved Forests, but now they are not allowed to touch them due to the fear of repraisals. The saplings of *mahua* mango and jack fruits are now planted by the Hill Korwa in their home-steads in almost all Korwa villages. Such trees are considered as household property. Rakaiya had the distinction of owning a pomegranate tree which was planted by a Forest Guard who stayed in the village years ago. The fruit was untouched by the people as they were not sure of its taste. But no sooner they tasted, they took great Kare of it. Now the tree belongs to the entire village. Children are specially fond of this tree and never forget to pour a pitcher of water at it during summer.

Agricultural Activities

The Hill Korwa in the past used to raise mustard, gram, maize, *rahar, til, kurti, jantgi, minijhri, madua* and *serali* in their *beora* fields for domestic consumption. Now the people complain that the yield has gone down and whatever the amount they grow can somehow meet their requirements for four or five moths only.

The crops raised by the people after abolition of shifting cultivation are oil seeds (*lotni* and *jantgi*), millets of inferior quality (*madia, gondli minjhlt, betha hudoo* pulses *serali*) *kurti* and *rahar*), *paddy*, and (*maize jonhri*).

Oil seeds

Lotni is a variety of mustard. Ploughing for the crop is carried out in the month of Kartik (October-November). This is followed by breaking of clods. Then sowing starts and is completed within a month. The crop is harvested in the month of Magh (January-February). Thrashing is carried out by men who beat the ears with a pole. The operation is known as *gedat ultijata.* Winnowing (*dauri*) is done by women. The beaten mixture of grains and straw is put in a winnowing fan which is raised over-head by both hands and the mixture is allowed to fall on the ground slowly. The wind separates straw from grain. Due to weight the grains fall directly on the ground and the straw is blown little away by the wind and keeps piling up. The grains are put in a bamboo basket (*tokni*).

Jantgi seed is black in colour. In shape it is like cummin seeds but bigger in size. Ploughing for *Jantgi* is carried out in the month of Bhadon (August-September) and sowing is completed by the end of Kuar (September October). Harvesting is done in the month of Magh (January-February). The method of thrashing is similar to that of *lotni*.

Paddy

Paddy is of two types : (1) *Gora* paddy and (2) *Beetha Hudoo* or paddy. *Gora* paddy is sown by transplantation method. The fields for *gora* paddy are situated near the source of irrigation as it requires more water than *beetha hudoo*. Seeds are sown in a nursery. Seedlings are plucked when they become4 to 5 inches long and are bound in sheaves by men. The sheaves are then taken for transplantation to the field. Transplantation is done by women. The Hill Korwa believe that women can remain in bending posture for a longer period than men can do. Men, on the other hand, supply sheaves of plants to women for transplantation. Transplantation of paddy is completed in the month of Bhadon (August-September) and the crop is harvested in Kartik (October-November).

Gora hudoo is not popular among the people because of the lack of suitable land (*kiyari*) and irrigation resources. Another reason given by the people was that the *handi* (beer) prepared from it is not as tasty as that of *beetha hudoo*. Harvesting is done both by men and women. Thrashing is done by pounding the ears with feet (*Katde Bointa*).

The *beetha hudoo* is sown by broadcasting method in the months of Jeth and Asadh (May to July) and is harvested in the month of Kartik (October-November). The *beetha hudoo* does not require much water for irrigation and makes a tasteful *handi* (beer). Thus, it is perferred by the people inspite of its low yield in comparison to *gora hudoo* (transplanted paddy).

Millets

Gondli is of two types : (1) *minijhri* and (2) *gudlo beetha* or *bhadaiya gondli*. It is sown in the month of Asadh (June July) and is harvested in the month of Aghan (November-December). *Bhadaiyan gondli* is cultivated in the black soil but *minjhri* can be grown in rocky soil. *Bhadaiyan gondli* is liked by the people because of its softness and high yield.

A person does not feel hungry for a longer period after eating this variety once and it requires more time for digestion. Its de-husked grains are boiled and eaten as rice. Very few Hill Korwa cultivate paddy, thus rice is considered as an item of luxury.

Another variety of millet is *madia.* It grows on rocky land *parti* and is sown in the month of Asadh (June-July) and harvested in Aghan (November-December). Thrashing is done by pounding the ears with feet (katde bointa). Cakes are prepared from its flour or the de-husked grains are boiled and eaten.

There are three varieties of *serali* or *berre.* (1) *Danr serali* (2) *Raidoo serali* and (3) *Jhampo serali. Radioo serali* is sown only in *beora* fields. Now it is grown no more. The only varieties the people cultivate are *danr serali* and *jhampoo serali. Danr serali* is grown in rocky fields. It is sown in Asadh (June-July) and harvested in Kuar (September-October). *Jampoo serali* is considered inferior than the *raidoo* and *danr serali.* The grains are hard and cakes can be made with difficulty. It cannot be eaten as it upsets the stomach. Baked *danr serali* is soft. It is sweet in taste and may be eaten boiled as well as baked in the from of bread. Thrashing is done by feet (Katde bointa).

Lentils

Kurthi is sown in the month of Asadh (June-July) and is harvested in Pous (December-January). Thrashing is done by bullocks and the operation is called *dauri. Rahar* is sown in the month of Jeth (May-June) and is harvested in Aghan (November-December). Lentils harvested by plucking the ears only. *Kurthi* straw, which helps the land to rejuvenate its fertility is allowed to rot in the field while new sprouts come out of *rahar* stumps in next season. Thus only pods of *Kurthi* and *rahar* are plucked. Sowing for *rahar* is done in alternate years.

Maize

Maize is eaten in the form of baked cakes, boiled broth and parched. The parched grains are called *loi,* which forms the evening refreshment of the people. There are two varieties of maize : (a) *Khatang* or *Jinhor* and (b) *Kutki*. Both of them are sown in Asadh (June-July). *Kutki* is an early variety of maize and is harvested in Kuar (September-October) while *Jinhor* is harvested a month later in Kartik (October-November) *Kutki* is preferred by the people as it makes good *lai* and is sweet in taste. The grains of *khatang* are bigger than *Kutki* and its yield is high. It makes good cakes. The ears are plucked from the stump and are pounded with wooden poles. The ears burnt during winters and stumps are given to animals.

Maize, mustard, tobacoo, and vegetable are sown in *bari*, a plot of land attached with the household. As *bari* lands are near the habitation, the people can take good care of it and protect it from wild animals. Intensive manuring of *bari* lands help good yield.

Mustard and *Jantgi* are mainly cash crops and supplement the income for cash transactions. Tobacco is grown in little quantities for self consumption. Tobacco leaves are plucked and drien in sun. The dried leaves are eaten after mixing with lime as an intoxicant and the mixture is called *khaini*.

It is apparent from the above description that the Hill Korwa produce a single crop. Most of sowing operation is performed by the end of June and the first crop of millets come not earlier than October. The harvesting of most of the crops is finished by the end of January. The agricultural products hold the people only till the May end. From June to October the Hill Korwa face semi-starvation situation as they are unable to save even seeds for sowing in the next season.

In Maltipur and Sardapath a few Korwa households cultivate black gram but most of the crop is eaten before ripening of grains. None of the Korwa households reported storage of gram. Rakaiya and Bansajhal were found without any gram. in Bansajhal, however, the village was observed to have cultivated little quantities of *alsi* and *til* (oil seeds).

Nature and economy

The deities which are worshipped by the Hill Korwa are the part of environment in which they live. The motives behind worship are centred around improving economic resources and keeping a sound health which is again essential for eking out a livelihood. Natural phenomena viz., lightning, drought, famine and epidemics provide an added pressure to seek supernatural help through worship of deities of spirits. The religious life of the people thus revolves round various rituals. The Hilll Korwa are extremely concerned about their health. A person with weak body and fragile health can hardly maintain himself and other members of his household. An ailing person receives little assistance from his household or kindred and is left on the mercy of others. Ailments paralyse all economic activities. The only alternative to avert this crisis is to make the deities and guardian spirits happy through offerings of chicken liquor (*daru*), and home made beer (*handi*). *Pirdoes* are a class of spirits responsible for a number of diseases and are worshipped on different occasions during different parts of the year as shown in the table on the following page.

The various occasions on which the above deities, as shown in Tables 4.2 and 4.3 are worshipped are Nava or Navagrahi, Kathori, Deothan, Cherta Amass and Haryari. They are described below.

Nava or Navagrahi

The word *nava* means 'new' as it is observed after harvesting of new millets in the month of Kuar (August-September). A chicken is sacrificed by the *dewar* and blood of the sacrificed chicken is mixed in millets or rice produced from the new crop. The chicken's meat is cooked with *papaya* (*mewa*) and eaten by members of the household. At night all villagers perform *karma* dance till the break of dawn. The blood mixed food grains are kept inside the inner room in a leafy container (*ponti*). Husband and wife in a household dedicate these *pontis* to their own deities who are considered to protect the two and other members of the household from illness. The *Ponti* is replaced during the next *nava* festival and its ingredients are cooked and eaten by the children of pre-puberty age, who are considered free from pollution.

TABLE 4.2

Worship of Pir Deo

Name of Deities	Occasion for worship	Month (English equivalent)	Reason for worship	Nature of worship
Sigirdeo/Shikarideo Dulhadeo/Bughwait	Nava	Kuar (August-September)	Protection against ailment	Individual household
Goradeo	Nava	-do-	Protection against boils	-do-
Bijri deo	Nava	-do-	Protection against lightning	-do-
Bhaloo deo	Nava	-do-	Protection against bears	-do-
Mahadeo/ Mahadevi	Kathori & Deothan	Baisakh (April—May) Aghan (January-February)	Protection of village against epidemics, drought, famine, for a bumper mahua flowerage	Collective Individual households
Baghori	Cherta	Magh (December-January)	Protection against tigers	

Other deities worshipped for enhancement of wealth through bumper cıop have been described in the following table.

TABLE 4.3

Worship of Deities Responsible for Higher Yield

Name of Deities	Occasion for Worship	Month (English equivalent)	Reason of Worship	Nature of rituals
Dhan Barinda/ Dhan Badhauna, Ann Barhaura, Ann Barinda,	Nava	Knar (August-September)	For enhancing wealth and economic affluence	Individual households
Lakmi	Amass	Aghan (October-November)	Protection and prolife-ration of cow and cattle	-do-
Pitar-deo	Haryari	Sawan (June-July)	Abundance of green leaves for consumption of men and animals. Protection against snakes and centi-pedes.	-do-

Kathori

Kathori is observed collectively by the villagers in the month of Baisakh (April-May) in honour of Mahadeo or Mahadani, who is implored to give a bumper crops of *mahua* flowers. Rituals are performed under a *mahua* tree. First of all the Baiga lits fire in the village reciting incantations and throwing some rice in the fire. Villagers carry the fire in a procession under the *mahua* tree which is supposed to be the abode of Mahadani and all the rituals are performed there. A chicken is offered to the deity. Before the sacrifice is made a handful of rice is served to the bird. Eating of rice by the bird is a sign acceptance by Mahadani of the sacrifice and if the bird is frightened and refuses to eat the rice, a few more chickens are promised by the Baiga to Mahadani. No sooner the bird starts eating the rice its throat is cut by an axe in a single blow. The blood which oozes out from the throat is made to fall on twelve small lumps of rice. The priest puts a gory mark on his forehead. The sacrificed chicken is cooked and is distributed among the participants. The rice is left in an open basket near the tree for consumption of rats and birds.

As said earlier Katori is observed collectively by all households of the village, the Kotwar of the village collects contribution from respective households at the rate of half a rupee or a chicken in lieu of it. The amount thus received is spent on purchase of chickens and rice for the feast and bottles of liquor for the priest who performs the ritual.

Deothan

Deothan is observed in the month of Magh (December-January) in the honour of Sigirdeo for economic prosperity of the household where Sigirdeo worship is performed two days prior to Deothan, the priest and his pupil (Dewar and Chelas) go on fast. On the day of Deothan the Chelas break their fast at the residence of the Dewar and are served with meals by the latter. The villagers prepare *handi* and offer individually to the Dewar who in return offers the drink to his *chelas*.

It was reported from Rakaiya that at the time of village settlement, the iron chain (*jarib*) used for measuring land had broken down twice. The Dewar attributed the phenomenon to the fury of Sigirdeo, who, was unhappy with the Hill Korwa becoming settled agriculturists. The frightened Dewar promised to offer 10 chickens to Sigirdeo and the offer appeased the deity. Afterwards the boundaries of the village were measured successfully. Since then the Hill Korwa of Rakaiya perform the worship of Sigirdeo collectively. In 1970, another land settlement was in the offing, Hence, the villagers performed the worship of Sigirdeo collectively at Rakaiyatla the supposed abode of the deity. One male member from each household of the village took part in the celebrations. Two chickens were sacrificed on the spot. Later the meat of the sacrificed chickens was cooked and eaten by the villagers. After these rituals, the Baiga and Dewar of the village were taken to the *bhatti* and offered liquor in return of their services.

In the past, when the Hill Korwa were *beora* cultivators, the Sigirdeo worship was performed by individual household at a larger scale. The invitation used to go round Korwa village. The host used to serve meals and drinks to all participants for a period ranging from 15 days to one month.

The mode of performing Sigirdeo worship was to erect a pole in front of the host's house fitted with a broom-stick on its top and decorated with peacock feathers. The worshippers used to sing hymns in praise of the deity round the clock. Four empty pitchers were usually kept on the ground under the pole. It is a common belief that on the last day of worship the pitchers would be filled with food grains dropped from the broom-stick attached with Sigirdeo's pole. It symbolised that the persons in whose auspices worship was performed will receive a bumper crop and those who had drunk the *handi* prepared from the contents of the sacred pitchers would also be benefited the blessings of Sigirdeo. After the abolition of *beora* cultivation, the people perform the worship of Sigirdeo collectively. The villagers of Maltipur and Sardapath reported that instead of performing Sigirdeo worship annually, they perform it after every six years in the old fashion.

Cherta

The term Cherta is derived from *sirana* or the end. Cherta is observed after completion of the agricultural year in the month of Magh December January). The Hill Korwa perhaps have borrowed this festival from the Oraons and Ghasis who observe this with great pomp and zest. The Oraon and Ghasi young boys and girls move from one village to another in batches playing drums, singing and dancing. It is customary on the part of each household to donate food grains to them. The food grains thus collected are cooked at one place and is eaten by members of the *cherta* team.

Among the Hill Korwa only boys constitute the cherta team. No Cherta team visited Rakaiy a during this investigator's stay in the village.

Amass

Amass is celebrated in the month of Aghan (January-February) in the honour to Lakhmi, the Goddess of wealth. On the day of Amass, the cow-sheds (*gaihar*) are cleaned and cows are served with special maize fodder. The caretaker boys are given a rupee or two or a *dhoti* (lion-cloth). A chicken is sacrificed for Lakhmi in each *gaihar* early in the morning. After night meals the villagers perform *karma* dances.

Haryari

After ffrst monsoon showers in the month of Asadh (June-July) Haryari is observed by each household exhorting the *pitar-deo* (ancestral spirits) to protect members of the household from bites of snakes, scorpions, and centipedes. Green leaves are cooked and eaten. A little amount of rice is offered to *pitar-deo* and is kept unguarded inside the sleeping room to be consumed by rats. The ancestral spirits are implored for a thick vegetation in the village and forest so that both men and animals are benefited by luxuriant growth

Jali

It has been reported earlier that the Hill Korwa were unchallenged masters of forests in their past. As the time passed their rights over the forest and its produces were considerably reduced by the encroachment of outsiders. But the tribe reacted against such encroachments and tried to establish its rights on the forest. Jali bears evidence of the Korwa right over forests.

The Hill Korwa have a strong sense of belongingness to the surrounding forests where most of deities have their respective abode. Hence the movement of other tribes in such forest tracts, which once belonged to the Hill Korwa, is resented upon by them lest the deities residing in the forest unleash their curses on the people. These forest deities should therefore, be appropriately propitiated and implored. The Hill Korwa, therefore. resent to perform rituals on behalf of other tribal groups who exploit forests which once belonged to the former. Performance of rituals involve some expenditure which the Hill Korwa of Rakaiya realise for the Kawars of Sarnadih. The amount realised from the Kawars is at the rate of seven kgs of paddy for each of the 30 households of Rakaiya.

The Kawars pay the levy willingly lest they should not be allowed by the Hill Korwa of Rakaiya to exploit forest produces.

From the above description it becomes clear that the Hill Korwa are not idlers getting all their needs satisfied by the bountiful nature. On the contrary, they lead an extremely difficult life. Their life revolves round the activities of food quest. It is, however, true that whatever resources they wrest from nature are not fully utilised by them for themselves. Non-tribal groups and other agencies usurp their resources leaving them high and dry without any food for atleast six months a year.

REFERENCES

1. Allee, E. M. 1949. *Principles of Animal Ecology*, Philadelphia, W.B. Saunders: 1.

2. Herskovits, M. J. 1952. *Economic Anthropology*, New York, Alfred and Knopf: 88.

CHAPTER FIVE

Economic Relationship

The Hill Korwa do not have a self-sufficient economy. The group interact with other communities in their day-to-day economic activities. The *grihat*, being employers provide the Hill Korwa with job opportunities. There are dealers from whom people get articles of day-to-day consumption. The debtor land them money from time to time and the *jajman* (Ghasia and Chamar) serve them at selected occasions. They share the produces of their land with another who invests inputs in land and becomes a tenant. This net-work of relationships operates at various levels.

The relationship between a *grihat* and a *harwaha* may be termed as employer-employee relationship. The employers are both tribals and non-tribals. The Oraons and the Bihari Muslims may be mentioned as examples. The Bihari Muslims came to Surguja from Palamu District of Bihar as petty traders with clothes, blankets and spices etc., to transact their business on the barter basis with the Hill Korwa. This was about 100 years ago. With the abolition of shifting cultivation, the Hill Korwa and Nagesia were left without any substantial means of livelihood and their economy received a shattering jolt. Both of these tribes rose in rebellion against the then ruler of Surguja. In order to quell the Korwa and Nagesia rebellion and also in order to put these people under effective administrative control, the ruler of Surguja thought it expedient to encourage the Muslims traders to settle in Surguja. He gave them land and appointed them as *gauntia* for collection of land revenue. The Bihari Muslims are found around Samri Tehsil of Surguja District side by side with the Nagesia, the Hill Korwa, and the Kawar. The virgin forests and land of Surguja attracted the Ahir of Mirzapur (U. P) in larger numbers who came with their cow-herds and settled down. Soon they emerged as prominent agriculturists. The Ahir,thus, started living side by side with the Hill Korwa throughout Surguja and Raigarh Districts.

In Rakaiya, the Hill Korwa work as the *harwaha* of the Bihari Muslims. In Maltipur, Oraon, Nagesia, and Ahir and in Bansajhal and Sardapath the Ahir alone engage them as *harwaha.*

Failure to attend the work upto the satisfaction of the master on the part of a *harwaha* is the main irritant between his and his master's relationships. Sometimes a *harwaha* may fail to attend to his duties due to some inevitable circumstances which invariably results in the *grihat's* wrath. One such incident involving a *grihat* and three brothers was observed at Rakaiya. Two of them were belaboured and were kept in illegal confinement. Angered by the *grihat's* attitude, the villagers of Rakaiya decided to cease working for their masters. The village was then raided by Siddiq Mian and his followers of Mahuadih. Nadiha's cow was taken away by the raiders because Nadiha had contract to extend one year's labour. He had received from Siddiq Mian Rs. 60/- and 5 maunds of maize on loan. On another occasion he got a loan of Rs. 80/- from his master. The *grihat* claimed Rs. 80/- and interest at the rate of 50% per annum. Similarly Duggi was also under contract to extend one year's labour and was given Rs. 100/- (Rs. 40/- in lieu of 5 maunds of food grains). The raider found nothing in his house except a *sari* and made good with it. Nanka, another *harwaha* sold his only bullock and paid back the money hc received in advance for full year's labour.

The *harwahas* complained bitterly about the arduous nature of their job. The landowning *harwahas* get very little or no time to attend their own fields. As a result of this preoccupation with the *grihat*, their own crops remain neglected resulting into a lower yield. The main contention of landless *harwahas* was that Rakaiya had sufficient forest lands to meet their food requirements but they are unable to exert themselves in clearing and levelling up forest land due to paucity of time.

The *grihats* on the other hand complain about the changing attitude of the *ha wahas* who are no more honest workers and are always after extracting money from the former. The *grihats* alleged that the Korwa labourers stop working at slightest pretexts. Thus, the only tactics to deal with the Hill Korwa labourers is to apply physical force. Bari Mian of Mahuadih said, "We treat the Pahari Korwa as our own children. Will not you thrash your child if he misbehaves". The patel of Mahuadih, who is a Kewat by caste and lives nearby, alleged that the Muslim *grihats* encourage the Hill Korwa to steal the cattle of their neighbours and provoke them to kill and eat cows. They also entice the Hill Korwa to steal corps of their neighbourers, and sell to the former at cheaper prices. This has made the Hill Korwa professional thieves and cattle lifters in the eyes of their neighbourers. The Muslim *grihats* complained that the Patel of Mahuadih and others (Hindus) incite the Hill Korwa not to work for Muslim *grihats*, lest the latter become more prosperous. Bari Mian of Pendardih made the following allegation.

"Sarjoo Patel (of Mahuadih village) and Naval Ram (Head of Hargawan Statutory Panchayat) want us to leave this place. They spare no opportunity to harass us. They incite the Hill Korwa to work against our interest. When Koka (a Korwa labourer of Rakaiya working for Muslim *grihats*) was murdered, they tried to implicate us. Sarjoo bribed (deceased) Koka's father Phauda to name my brother Asghar Patel (of Mahudih) as the main conspirator but Phauda refused to do so as his generations have been eating our *namak* (salt)".

The Hill Korwa therefore, are the victim of the inherently tense relationship between the Bihari Muslims and Hindus but both of them unitedly derive maximum benefits from the

Korwa Labourers of Rakaiya. The Hill Korwa, however, suffer from a dilemma. They adore the Hindu brethren because of their religious affinities but are almost entirely dependent on the Muslims for fulfilment of their day to day economic needs. Konds of Patratoli worked as a *harwaha* in the farm of a prominent Kawar and a member of the Legislative Assembly. At the time of his marriage, he demanded the payment of arrears from his *grihat*. But his request was rejected on some ground or the other. As a result, Konda's parents expressed their incapability to spend for their son's marriage. Ultimately Ronha of Rakaiya bore all expenditure of his step-daughter's marriage with Konda against the usual custom in which it is the son's father's obligation to bear such expenses.

In Maltipur, Korwa labourers work with the Oraons and Nagesias. Here the relationship between the labourers and masters appeared relatively better but on further probe the Hill Korwa complained about arduous nature of job, long hours of duty, tardy payments of wages, and lack of leave benefits.

In Bansajhal, the Hill Korwa worked for Bhola Mehto (Ahir) in the past but their relationship became strained after Bhola Mahto got a decree over the Hill Korwa land. As a result of tense relations with the Hill Korwa, Bhola stopped recruiting Korwa labourers of Bansajhal and engaged farm labourers from other villages. Now, the Hill Korwa do not work for Bhola Mehto. This has caused further hardships to the people.

In Sardapath, as mentioned earlier, the Korwa labourers work for the Mahatos (Ahirs). Relationship between the two groups is relatively better, but not without strains. The Korwa labourers feel bitter about the high handedness of the *grihats*, who do not grant the Hill Korwa one day's leave after every nine days of work. If a labourer fails to attend his work, he is subjected to humiliation and intimidations. Early in the morning, batches of Mahatos roam about the village and exhort their respective *harwahas* in abusive languages to go for work.

Few Hill Korwa in Sardapath are sometimes employed by their own kinsmen as agricultural labourers. Harya Ram of Sardapath had employed the son of Talhoo Ram who was working in order to save money for his marriage. Talhoo Ram told that the terms offered by Harya Ram were no better than those of the Mahto *grihats*.

An important aspect of *harwa-grihat* economic relationship is in the form of dealer-consumer relationship. Originally trader and cattle raisers, the Bihari Muslims and Ahirs, emerged as dominant landlords of their respective areas and also became traders. Thus the role of *grihat* changed from cultivators to petty dealers. The Bihari Muslims, now, run liquor shops throughout Surguja. They also run small shops for the local tribals. The commodities kept by them in their shops are mill-made clothes, raw-tobacco, jaggery, food grains, torches, torch cells, tea, salt, spices, condiments, cigarettes, indigenous cigars (biri) and earthern wares (purchased from Kumbhars). Muslim vendors roam about in Korwa villages with commodities of immediate consumption like spices, butter-milk, vegetables and raw tobacco. Vendors and shopkeepers insist on barter transactions with the Hill Korwa and thus extract huge margins of profit. The barter rates of few selected articles prevailing in Rakaiya, Maltipur, Bansajhal, and Sardapath have been shown in the Table 5.11.

It is evident from Table 5.11 that the Hill Korwa suffer heavy losses in barter transactions. A dried leaf of tobacco worth Re. 00.25 in local markets is bought by the Hill Korwa against 2 kgs of millets worth Re.00.50. The percentage of loss suffered by the consumer (Hill Korwa) is100. Similarly a bottle of liquor can be had for Re. 1.00 only at the bhatti (brewery) but the Hill Korwa obtain it by giving away 15 kgs of rice or 5 kgs of millets worth Rs. 1.50 and Rs. 2.50 respectively. As said earlier millets constitute the staple diet of the people and hence very few Hill Korwa can afford to get liquor against rice. The extent of loss suffered in bartering liquor against rice is 50 per cent and against millets 150 per cent. The dual nature of profit in barter, it appears, has been evolved by the owners of the *bhahtis* to extract maximum

TABLE 5.1

Barter Rate In Korwa Villages

Articles received in barter			Articles given in barter			
Name of articles	Quantity	Price at Market (in Rs.)	Name of articles	Quantity	Price at Market (in Rs)	Percentage of loss
Tobacco	1 leaf	00.25	Millet	2 kgs	00.50	100 00
Biri	1 packet	00.30	-do-	2 kgs	00.50	66.67
Butter Milk	1 litre	03.20	Rice	12 kgs	00.50	150.00
Spices	1 packet	00.10	Millet	2 kgs	00.50	400.00
Liquor	1 bottle	2.00	Rice/	1.5 kgs	1.50	50.00
			Millet	5 kgs	2.50	150.00

from the people who are least aware of the worth of their produces. Other advanced tribals and caste Hindus neither depend on millets as staple diet nor would like to suffer huge losses due to their relatively better awareness of prices in local as well as regional markets. The Hill Korwa are yet to develop market awareness. Ahir vendors, both male and female, go from one village to another with pitchers of butter-milk about the cost of which the latter is least aware. The market price of one litre of butter-milk (*mattha*) is Re. 00.20 but a Ahir vendor demands and gets 1/2 kg of rice from the Hill Korwa worth Re. 00.50 in the local markets thus making a profit of 150 per cent. The margin of profit gained on a packet of spices is the maximum. The packet contains a small quantity of chillies, turmeric and *dhanya* powder which can be purchased for 10 paisas from local markets but for the same packet a Hill Korwa gives away 2 kgs of millets worth Re. 00.50. Thus, the quantum of loss suffered by him is 400 per cent.

Indebtedness

Loans taken in the form of food grains and/or cash money are known as *derhwa*, a term derived from the Hindi word *derh* meaning 'one and a half' because the rate of interest on all such loans is 50 per cent per annum. If a person takes Rs. 10/- on loan, he is required to return Rs. 15/- in the next year and so on. Hence even a little sum taken on loan becomes an intolerable burden within a couple of years.

Borrowing of money and food grains are perpetually resorted to by the people in order to meet everyday needs. As the popular saying goes, a Hill Korwa is born in debt, lives in debt and dies in debt. The *grihats* keep a vigilant eye on the people and land them money and food grains generously. Bari Mian of Pendardih claimed: "During 1968 famine the Collector ordered us to see that not a single Pahari Korwa dies of hunger in Rakaiya. We gave them food as much as they wanted and thus blocked a considerable amount of our money. Now, when they are reaping their harvests, they refuse to return us the loan". The *grihats*, however, realise their loans with ferocity, ruthlessness and cruelty. Band of *grihats* were seen roaming about in the village at the time of harvest realising old debts. In some cases it was reported that standing crops were forcibly harvested by the *grihats* depriving the people of their major source of food supply.

Ronha of Rakaiya borrowed Rs. 10/- from a *grihats*. When the former wanted to refund money with interest at the rate of 50 per cent per annum, the *grihats* refused to accept money and instead demanded and got 15 kgs of *Jantgi*, worth Rs. 25/- in the local market.

In a village of Jonkapath Hills, this investigator saw a Muslim trader beating a Hill Korwa. On investigation he was told that the belaboured Korwa took on loan 5 kgs of *dalya* (oats of vulgar wheat) from the trader, who demanded Jantgi instead of actual article given on loan. The Korwa refused to pay Jantgi with interest and hence got the thrashing. It is interesting to mention here that *dalya* is one of the articles distributed free of cost to the Hill Korwa through Primary School teachers by the CARE. The article seems to have reached to the trader through a school teacher, who was sharing a portion of the trader's house, who seized an opportunity to distribute the article in question among the femished Hill Korwa on loan without making any investment, of his own.

The following table shows the extent of indebtedness among the Hill Korwa of the four villages under study.

TABLE 5.2

Indebtedness Among The Hill Korwa

Name of the Village	Total No. of households	No. of households in debt	Percentage
Rakaiya	30	18	60.00
Maltipur	23	13	56.52
Bansajhal	36	21	58.33
Sardapath	60	41	68.33
Total	149	93	62.42

It is evident from Table 5.2 that 62.42 per cent of Korwa households are indebted to *grihats* only. The highest rate of indebtedness of 68.33 per cent was reported from Sardapath followed by Bansajhal where 58.33 per cent households were in debt. In Rakaiya the proportion of indebtedness was found 60 per cent and in Maltipur it was 56.52 per cent.

Some of the Hill Korwa drink liquor (*daru*) on loan. The terms of the loan are similar to those mentioned above. The quantity of liquor is converted into money and the rate of interest is calculated on the basis of the quantity of liquor given to the consumer. It was found that the Hill Korwa are lured to drink by the *bhattidars* (owners of breweries). The unwilling drinkers are some times threatened and intimidated. They are not allowed to brew their traditional drink (*handi*) at home.

The *bhattidars* have unlawfully opened shops for selling liquor in Korwa villages which are known as *gaddi*. Such establishments are invariably run by fellow villagers on commission basis. The vendor is given 10 bottles free of cost if he sells 42 bottles. Thus, the commission paid to a *gaddidar* by the *bhatidiar* is 22.76 per cent. The Hill Korwa who runs a *gaddi* either invariably drinks more than his permissible quota or spend the money received from sale on himself instead of handing it over to the *bhattidar.*

Talhoo Ram of Sardapath used to run a *gaddi* in his house. He failed to check the temptation of liquor and over drank. As a result of this, he failed to return the agreed amount of money to the *bhattidar.* Talhoo Ram's wife's brother also committed the same mistake. Consequently his house was raided by the *bhattidar* and a bullock and two cows were forcibly taken away by him. Smelling the danger Talhoo Ram fled from the village with his wife and children leaving his cattle in the custody of one of his kinsmen. He was not traceable when this author left the village.

Mortgage

Drinks are also made available on mortgage of land, household articles, and cattle. During this author's stay at Rakaiya,

Tangra Korwa, the Red Turban Chief of the area confessed that he had mortgaged his Red Turban for a sum of Rs.2/- with the *bhattidar*. It was given to him by Police Department. In the meantime he was called at Shankargarh Police Station for investigations in connection with a theft case. He was quite upset about how to go to the Police Station without the turban.

Mortgage is known as *bandha*. It is resorted to for borrowing substantial amounts of money. The terms of mortgage are of two different kinds. One is known as *banpha* and the other is called *bura bandha*. According to the former, until repayment of the entire amount of loan for all practical purposes, the creditor becomes the owner of the land that has been mortgaged to him. "...*bura bandha* system, according to which a fixed amount of money is deducted from the total amount of loan every year. By making such deductions when the whole amount is repaid the land is returned to its original owner. In this dyadic relationship the tribals are always the debtors and the non-tribals are the creditors".[1]

The Hill Korwa do not go for *bura bandha*. The creditors are not generous to allow this automatic settlement nor the Hill Korwa are literate enough to know about the legal aspects of such transactions. The need for money becomes urgent in case of sudden eventualities and life cycle rituals. The relationship between creditors and debtors are quire smooth in the beginning but ends with breach of confidence, latent hostility, and mutual distrust. It was repeatedly alleged by the Hill Korwa informants that the creditors fail to keep promise. Lands were not returned to the land owners even after making full payment of the loan. In several cases the creditors refused to accept the repayment of loan in order to enjoy the mortgaged land as long as possible. A few such cases are stated below.

1. Lohra of Kotli village (Surguja) mortgaged 4 acres of land to Brij Raj Ahir seven years ago for a sum of Rs. 60/-. Lohra had paid the amount but the land was not returned to him.

2. Dhoopan, of Barpani village (Surguja) mortgaged a plot of land in which the yield was stated to be 60 maunds

per year, to a Kawar of Pahri village three years ago. Dhoopan claimed that he had returned the money but the creditor had refused to vacate the said land. Dhoopan took up the matter with the land revenue authorities who promised to look into the matter. In the meantime they asked Dhoopan to cultivate the disputed plot of land. Dhoopan cultivated the land accordingly but the creditor stopped him from reaping the harvest.

Lack of agricultural inputs and irrigation facilities rather than excess land forces a Hill Korwa to give land on share-cropping (*batai*) either to one of his own kin or to his tribal brethren or the non-tribal neighbours. A Hill Korwa has been treated in this set of relationship as the landowner and one with whom he enters into *batai* relationship as a tenant. Such relationship may be termed as landowner-tenant relationship. The system of *batai* is of two types. The first system is known as *sajha*. In this the landowner supplies seeds in addition to the land and the share-cropper contributes human and bullock labour for cultivating the land. Two-thirds of the total yield is taken away by the landlord and one third is by the share-cropper. This system is almost absent among the Hill Korwa who are hardly able to save seeds until the time of sowing. In the second system, which is popularly known as *adha-batai*, the tenant supplies seeds and labour and receives a half of the total yield.

The *adha-batai* system has been modified for the Hill Korwa by the non-Korwa tenants who leave no opportunity to squeeze maximum benefits from the illiterate Korwa. The tenants demand ploughed land from the Hill Korwa to which the latter, always in great need of in-puts, concede even at a loss of labour in-put. Factors responsible for high frequency of share-cropping may be attributed to the following causes.

(i) Lack of agricultural in-puts viz., draught cattle, irrigation facilities, seeds, and right type of fertilizers.

(ii) Lack of interest in cultivation. It is culmination of the past practice of *bewar* which was the main method of cultivation. The *bewar* activities provided the people more adventure, thrill and entertainment, and settled agriculture proved to be less charming and a drab affair which people adopted rather hesitatingly. Lack of technical know-how involved in settled agriculture also made the Hill Korwa less inclined towards plough cultivation. As a result of this the people's dependence on forest and forest produces is still considerable.

(iii) As the *beora* was abolished without providing a suitable alternative to the people they developed an apathy towards plough cultivation and desisted from self-cultivation in large numbers.

Ceremonial Economic Relationships

Jali and *Cherta*, referred to earlier may be termed as ceremonialised economic relationship which the Hill Korwa maintain with their neighbours. Jali relationship may have developed due to dwindling of forest resources on which the Hill Korwa depend heavily. Continuous exploitation of forests by other tribes is resulting into their disappearance creating a problem of survival for the Hill Korwa. Hence, the latter, finding themselves unable to check the numerically and economically dominant tribes physically had adopted this mechanism to put up a deterrent against infringements of their traditional rights and over the forest wealth. In Maltipur, Bansajhal, and Sardapath, the system of *Jali* levy is present and the people give a different explanation for it. The Hill Korwa of these villages give an undertaking to the Mahtos, Oraons and Nagesia for protecting the latter's cattle and crops. Hence each Hill Korwa household is given 5 kgs of paddy in a year collectively by the Mahto, Oraon and Nagesia.

The Hill Korwa maintain economic relationship with the Ghasia and Chamar also. Both the Ghasia and Chamar are Scheduled Castes and consider themselves above the Hill Korwa in terms of commensality but the Ghasia accept liquor, *handi*, and uncooked food from the latter. The Korwa relationship with the Ghasia is more intimate than with that of the Chamar. The Ghasia are professional drummer, singers, dancers, and acrobats. They are invited by the Hill Korwa to perform singing and dancing at the time of *mangabara* or *biah*. A Ghasia party of dancers is susually given a fee of Rs. 10/- but the Ghasia prefer to receive goat skins from time to time from their Korwa clients for making drums (*mandar* and *daphla*). The Chamars lift dead cattle of the Hill Korwa and supply the owner of the cattle a pair of shoes. Now the traditional *jajmani* type of relationships are giving way to contractual transactions. The Hill Korwa pay the Ghasia in cash for the latter's performance. The Chamars pay cash money to the Hill Korwa for the hide of a dead animal and if a Korwa need a pair of foot wears, he purchases it from the Chamar by paying the latter price of the pair of shoes in cash. Besides these two above mentioned castes described above, no other castes or tribes of the area maintain *jajmani* type of relationship with the Hill Korwa.

Net-work of Economic Exploitation

Illiteracy coupled with ignorance and fear of outsiders have made the Hill Korwa an easy target of exploitation, which is resorted to by their own tribal brethren, non-tribal *grihats, Sahukars* or traders, *bhathi* and *gaddi* owners and the agents responsible for the planned social change of the Hill Korwa. A few illustrations have already been furnished and some more stated below will help finding the nature of relationship between the exploited Korwa and their exploiters.

(a) A villager in Rakaiya procured some wood from a dry tree fallen inside the village and shaped a pair of doors which could fetch him Rs. 30. The Forest Guard charged the villager by saying that the latter had removed the wood from the Reserved Forest. The Forest Guard demanded Rs. 35/- as his fee to hush up the matter. Left with no alternative the villager sold the finished door panel in Rs.30/- and borrowed Rs. 5/ from a kinsman and paid the demanded sum to the Forest Guard. Not only his labour had gone to a total waste but the said villager plunged still deeper into the abyss of indebtedness.

(b) During the 1970 Land Settlement, the Patwari of one of the four villages under study sent a message in the village that the settlement party had come and was going to measure land for allotment to the Hill Korwa. Hence each Korwa household was asked to bring five loads of wood at the Patwari's residence. Early in the morning, all Korwa men, women and children went to the forest and returned with head loads of fuel wood in the afternoon. The next day the entire amount of fuel wood was dumped in front of the Patwari's residence. The fuelwood had had nothing to do with the land-settlement but the Patwari called the villagers for completion of the voter's list for the mid-term parliamentary polls.

(c) The Hill Korwa of Khairadih (District Surguja) paid collectively a sum of Rs. 300/- to an advanced Survey party consisting of the members of revenue and forest departments. Members of the party demanded money from the villagers and threatened the unwilling Korwas of including their lands in the Reserved Forest.

(d) In Rakaiya, the Hill Korwa were given a plot of land named Rakaiya Taal at the time of rehabilitation of village in which the villagers raised three successive crops. The land was reported to be of good quality and very close to a natural stream. The *grihats* of the area claimed Rakaiya Taal under their possession and stopped the Hill Korwa to cultivate the same plot the following year. Thus a dispute arose and Rakaiya Taal remained fallow till it was included in the Reserved Forests by the land settlement of January 1970.

(e) Similarly, the Hill Korwa of Tangar Toli in Jonkapath region were given a plot of land in the forest for purposes of cultivation. The Mahtos and Nagesias made a joint representation against the said allotment and claimed that the plots a *gaochar* (pasture). They evicted the Hill Korwa from the land forcibly. It is worthwhile to mention here that one of the members of Mahto caste was the head of the statutory panchyat and his deputy belonged to the Nagesia tribe.

(f) A Hill Korwa of Kharkona (District Surguja) narrated the following story which helps us to understand the nature of the exploited and exploiters relationship.

"The land was duly possessed by my father. In a *nistar* (land settlement) my father submitted all the papers with the Tahsildar at Kusmi. When the papers were returned to their respective owners, the Mahto offered to collect them on my father's behalf and my father readily agreed to the proposal. The Mahto collected my father's papers but never returned them to their owner. When my father insisted for return of the same, the Mahto replied 'Do not keep the papers with you, they will be eaten away by rats or spoiled by smokes and rains. Let the papers be with me'. My father trusted the Mahto, who in return got my father's land transferred in his name".

(g) The following is the story of Hill Korwa of Bansajhal.

The Collector permitted them to reclaim a plot of land which they cleared by removing boulders and levelling the ground. When the fields were ready for cultivation, Bhola Mahto claimed the newly begotten land as his *naochar* (pasture). He filed a case in the Collector's Court at Ambikapur. The Hill Korwa having no pleader, could not contest the case. Ultimately Bhola Mahto brought a decree from the Court in his favour from the Court of Law and evicted them from the said tract of land which they made cultivable after putting great labour.

Besides the role of money lenders and traders the *grihats* play an additional role of middle-men between the Hill Korwa and the *Sahukars* (traders) of Marwar' and Haryana for extracting the agriculural produces. It has been said earlier that the *grihats*, advance to the Hill Korwa and in return attach their crops. It was found that the *grihats* are financed by the *Sahukars*, who run their business establishments relatively away from tribal villages. The modus operandi is as follows:

Grihats purchase Korwa crops and sell the same to the *Sahukars*. In return of money they receive from the latter after deducting their commission. The commission deducted by the *grihats* varies between 20% to 30%.

Local weekly markets provide another opportunity to the *grihats* to purchase food grains from the neighbouring tribes.

The *grihats* take their position early morning on all approach roads to the markets and scan the passersby includng the Hill Korwa. They try all their wits to stop the Korwa customer from going to the market with food grains. A Hill Korwa, generally sells away his commodity to the nearest available *grihat* partly as a matter of obligation and partly for avoiding the inconvenience of going to the market with head-loads. Even if an industrious Korwa reaches to the market he is easily spotted by the *Sahukars* who offer the former a lower price for his commodities than that offered by a *grihat*. The Hill Korwa, therefore, get no incentive for taking their produces to the market. The grihats, thus, play an intermediary role in flushing out agricultural produces from the Hill Korwa and handing it over to the *Sahukars* after making a substantial margin of profit.

Besides agricultural produces, the land of the Korwa are also taken away by the *grihats* inspite of restrictions imposed by the Government on purchase of tribal lands without permission of the Distrite authorities by non-tribals. The mode of grabbing Korwa land is described below.

A *Sahukar* advances money to a *grihat*. The *grihat* hires a tribal agent to take the Korwa land either on mortgage or on share-cropping. In course of time, the tribal agent succeeds in purchasing the Korwa land after little pursuation. Now the *grihat* and his tribal agent, who happens to be economically well off seek the District Collector's permission for the transfer of land from the tribal agent to the *grihat*. Once the land comes out of the tribal possession, it takes no time in reaching the hands of *Sahukar*, who earns a better profit from land by investing better in-puts. Thus, all good patches of Korwa lands have already gone out of the former's possession to the *grihats* and from *grihat* to *Sahukars*. However, the *Sahukars* do not maintain a direct economic relationship with the Hill Korwa. Instead, they reap benefits indirectly from the Korwa-*grihat* economic ties.

The nature of economic relationships between the Hill Korwa, their immediate neighbours, alien traders, and the direction of flow of Hill Korwa goods may be represented in the following diagram.

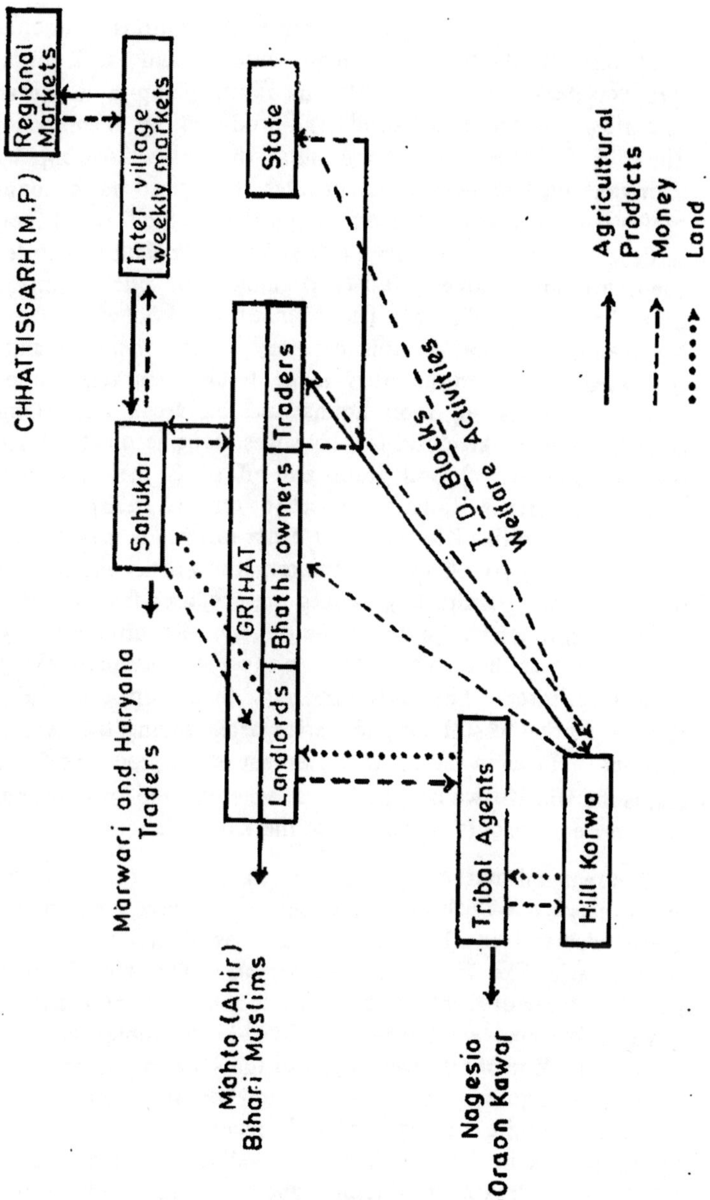
CHHATTISGARH (M.P)
Regional Markets
Inter village weekly markets
State
Sahukar
GRIHAT
Traders
Bhathi owners
Landlords
Blocks
I. D.
Welfare Activities
Marwari and Haryana Traders
Mahto (Ahir) Bihari Muslims
Tribal Agents
Hill Korwa
Nagesio Oraon Kawar
Agricultural Products
Money
Land

Diagram 5.1

In the diagram, rectangles represent various economic units through which Korwa land, money and agricultural products pass and these units in return pump-in money to the tribe. Agricultural products produced by members of the tribe find their way to *grihats* through sharecropping, mortgage, repayment of loans, or interest incurred on the loans which the Hill Korwa get from the *grihats* in the form of food grains. The *grihats* are given money by the *Sahukars* who are the traders and money lenders running their establishments away from tribal villages. The Marwari and *Sahukars* from Haryana may be put in this category. The *Sahukars* shift their establishment to the inter-village weekly markets temporarily for purchasing food grains and oil seeds and selling consumer goods like cloth, jaggery suges kerosine oil etc. After making purchases of good grains and oil seeds, they transport them to Kharsia in Raigarh District for onward transportation out of Chattisgarh. Kharsia and other rail heads may be put under the category of regional market. It is worthwhile to mention here that agricultural produces are procured from the Hill Korwa at throw away prices by the *grihats*, who, after realising their profit pass the same produces on to the *Sahukars* making them still dearer. The *Sahukars* pass them onward to the regional market at still a higher price after taking their share of profit. Hence in the entire movement of oil seeds and food grains the Hill Korwa are the losers whereas the *grihats* and *Sahukars* earn profits at the cost of the Korwa labour.

The regional market, thus pumps in money to the tribal sector in order to flush out its agricultural produces which are in great demand in the country. This is done through the intermediaries like *Sahukars* and *grihats*. The money thus earned by the Hill Korwa finds a way to the *grihat* who invariably runs business establishments like *bhatti* (liquor shops) and grocery. The *bhatti* owners pay to the state as a licence fee for running liquor shops. A portion of the money thus earned by the state through such licences is again spent on the Hill Korwa in form of various welfare activities. The Hill Korwa, in return spend their money on liquor and consumer goods.

The lands given by the state to the Hill Korwa find a way to the *grihats* through non-Korwa tribal agents with whom the Hill Korwa enter into land transactions through mortgage and sale and finally reaches the *Sahukars.*

It is evident, therefore, that the Hill Korwa have been reduced merely as recipient of money in return of their land and agricultural produces. With ever decreasing value of money, the Hill Korwa find themselves in a very difficult situation where even their minimum basic needs are fulfilled.

REFERENCES

1. Danda, A.K. 1977. "Tribal Situation in Northeast Surguja" in *Tribal Situation in Northeast Surguja*, Edited by A.K. Danda, Calcutta, Anthropological Survey of India : 4.

CHAPTER SIX

Changing Economy

The Hill Korwa practised shifting cultivation till 1867.[1] The sudden change over of their main source of livelihood left the people dazed and shocked. A part of the tribe turned itself into a gang of marauders which appeared to subsist altogether by pillage, which was not seldom accompanied by murder but for some years, they have been well conducted, the leaders having for the most part been induced to take up lands in the plains. This situation continued more or less unabated till 1952 when the feudatory state of Surguja and Raigarh were merged with the Indian Republic. The situation *beora* was reviewed and the Government decided that shifting cultivation should be allowed only in cases where people are solely dependent on this until such times as they will require to take to move to settled life. Simultaneously, efforts to rehabilitate the Hill Korwa in forest villages were made with little success.

The Hill Korwa, thus, entered from one economic system based on food gathering, hunting and shifting cultivation to the other based on settled agriculture and labour. The factors responsible for this transformation can be enumerated as follows :

(a) Abolition of shifting cultivation by law

(b) Changing of forest policies

(c) Development of transport and communication system

(d) Opening of liquor shops

Effects of change-over to settled agriculture

The change-over to settled agriculture is the most important factor contributing to break the self-sufficiency of the people's economy and their age old isolation. Now the Hill Korwa economy is a part of the regional economy of Chattisgarh. As shifting cultivators, the people's needs were limited which were being fully catered to by the forest. Men covered their private parts of the body with leaves and women with grass skirts. Many a Hill Korwa in Jonkapath (Surguja District) smelt iron and even now they do it for shaping their axes and arrow-heads, though majority of them purchase the above articles from iron-smiths. Being shifting cultutivators the Hill Korwa were not primarily a farmer depending completely on the vagaries of nature as they are now. In the past, they knew very well how to exploit forest resources to their maximum benefit. The items of their diet were varied. Fruits, roots and flowers were plentiful. Games were also abundant. When the Hill Korwa were forced to adopt settled agriculture they were not provided with the means of irrigation, proper type of land, and better input materials. The result was disastrous. The people killed and consumed the bullocks which were distributed free by the Government as draught animals. Seeds were given free but were never sown by people. Instead, they were eaten. Houses were provided to them but were deserted soon. The residents disappeared into thick forests along with the window and door panels of their newly begotten houses. These events earned the Hill Korwa the distinction of a measure of notoreity which boomaranged on the Korwa society in the form of greater economic hardships and deprivation. Under the changed circumstances, the people are always obsessed with the fear of food scareity. This fear complex has forced them to seek employment with local petty traders-cum-landlords (*grihat*). This, in return, keeps them occupied with and dependent on non-agricultural pursuits. As a result of their preoccupation, with the *grihat* they cannot fully concntrate on their own fields. This process draws a Hill Korwa deeper into the abyss of indebtedness. Consequently, he sells off all his land and becomes absolutely dependent on the *grihat*.

The agricultural practices of the Hill Korwa were intertwined with magic, religion and economic practices. Success in agriculture depended more on man and spirit relationships than on any other factor. Spirits were propitiated for a bumper harvest, success in hunting, a safe passage in the forests where the spirits would stupefy the beasts to such an extent that they would never notice a passing Hill Korwa. There are spirits to be worshipped for replenishment of food stock and wealth. In the past, all such spirits were worshipped on a large scale privately by the wealthy Hill Korwas in which the fellow tribesmen from nearby villages would also participate. Sigirdeo-*pooja* may be illustrated as an example. Now all such rituals including Sigirdeo-*pooja* have assumed the character of limited festivities and are celebrated collectively by all the villagers through their mutual contributions *Ghirra*, the famous fair-market of Chattisgarh, once attracted a large number of Hill Korwa participants. Now, very few of them participate in *ghirra* for want of resources and the festival has lost its significance for the Hill Korwa.

The Hill Korwa, like othes tribal groups, were characterised in the past by the mutual relationship of reciprocity. The *mukhya* (head of the village council of elders) used to select a tract of land for the entire community for carrying out *beora* cultivation. Hence land was held collectively. Members of respective households not only worked on their own plots but also would help others. Hence the spirit of the people in the past was the spirit of collective living and co-operation. When they started making their living through plough cultivation, the traditional spirit of co-operation and collectivity gave place to individualistic tendencies. Individual farmers are now, concerned about their respective fields, crops, and yield. In the spare time, an individual keeps himself busy in other pursuits which helps him to supplement the sources of livelihood. He has little or no time for helping others.

Sukkhan of Rakaiya, gave a portion of land to his son Biphna but not the bullocks. Biphna was serving a *grihat* as a labourer and purchased a bullock from his saving He was thinking to purchase another bullock after a few years. In Sardapath Talhoo Ram's son was working in the farm of another Korwa who was a member of the village council of elders (panchayat) Talhoo Ram always complained that his son is getting no good treatment from his own kinsman than that of the Mahto. The above examples show clearly that the old spirit of reciprocity and mutual co-operation which was once the tradition of the tribe is waning away. The sense of individualism has not only affected the group as a whole but this tendency is visible even within a household.

The Hill Korwa have nostalgic memories about the items of their diet which they were consuming as shifting cultivators. They used to grow in their *beora* fields diffeıent varieties of millets, maize, paddy, groundnuts, sweet-potatoes, sesame, mustard of two varieties and various types of pulses. Raidoo seralı, a millet was grown only in *beora* fields, and was famous for its tasty brew. Now this variety of millet is about to face extinction. Their diet was further supplemented by tubers, roots, and meat. Now, the people get little time for searching the above items. Nor are they free to move about in their quest. They mainly depend on whatever they produce. The consumption of meat, wild roots and tubers is also gradually declining. Women, who used to carry out gleaning in the forest now mostly remain engaged in farm operations. Game are also scarce, particularly due to stringent forest laws. Consequently, the Hill Korwa now depend mostly on cereal diet. Many Korwa informants told that their health is also declining. The people in the past could bend their bows to the U shape with a comparative ease and their arrow could traverse a longer distance. Now the Korwa are less healthier than their predecessors.

The change in system of cultivation is not only reflected in the Korwa diet but it has also given rise to new economic responsibilities of a regular cultivalor that the Hill Korwas were not used to. Now a Korwa has to pay a fixed amount of money to the Forest Department periodically for exploitation of forest produces. Regularly he has to satisfy the greedy petty officials also in the form of paying illegal gratification. For all these activities he needs money which he aquires either through sale of cash crops or labour. Limited amount of land under possession leaves little scope for raising crops at the cost of food grains which are not sufficient to fulfil his requirement even for five months in a year. In order to meet the increasing money liabilities, the Hill Korwa are either mortgaging or selling away their lands and consequently they are swelling the ranks of agrestic surfs.

Another significant change which has come about as a result of abolition of shifting cultivation is in the sphere to sexual division of labour. Under the old shifting cultivation pattern, hunting was mainly a male activity. Except in heavy and hazardous activities like hunting, climbing on trees, or felling them, women worked side by side with their men-folk. Both men and women used to carry out gathering activities collectively. The introduction of plough cultivation has distrubed this arrangement to some extent. Men, now, keep themselves busy in agricultural or labour activities without any break round the year. Hence they get little or no time to go to forest. Thus, the task of collecting forest produces has largely been left to women, with additional responsibilities in agricultural activities. Consequently, the Korwa family life is passing through a severe strain. Incidences of desertions and divorces have become more frequent.

The cost of in-put materials in settled agriculture is higher than in case of shifting cultivation. More seeds are required as sowing is done closely. Purchase and maintenance of draught cattle involve high expenditure. Even loaning a bullock for ploughing costs dearly. Hence for the fulfilment of such needs he resorts to further borrowing which erodes his already meagre economic resources.

As a result of the factors mentioned above, the Hill Korwa are weaning themselves away from plough cultivation and are leaning heavily towards cash transaction. The main source of cash is the land and labour.

Increasingly lands are either being mortgaged or given for a long spell of share-cropping. Once, alienated from the land, the people are adopting labourer's status in increasing numbers. A few Hill Korwa of Sardapath (District Kasgarh) had returned from the tea plantations of Assam and North Bengal. They have enthused the younger population of the village for migration to Assam. The less resourceful villagers of Rakaiya and Bansajhal work for their Muslim and Mahto *grihats* respectively.

Forest Policies and Exploitation of forest

The Hill Korwa were masters of the forest in the past. All that forests contained belonged to them. Under the Indian Forest Act 1927, the forest have been classified in the categories of reserved forests, protected forests, and village forests. The reserved forests are permanently retained and the Hill Korwa were not given any right over them. The people were permitted to exploit the forest product from protected forests on a nominal charge of Rs. 5/- per annum, per household. However the Korwa Hill had no right of felling trees. The implementation of National Forest Policy and the Forest Laws, therefore, vitally affected the economy of the Hill Korwa. The Hill Korwa were given rent free forest lands and their traditional *nistar* rights to graze their cattle in the forests were protected. Under the traditional *nistar* rights the Hill Korwa were permitted to collect fuel-wood, forest timber, and bamboo for own need for construction of their houses without any payment. However hunting has been declared as illegal in reserved and protected forests. No restrictions were imposed on hunting or trapping of small games. In respect of collecting minor forest produces the Hill Korwa were allowed by the Forest Department to collect *herra beherra* aonla, tamarind, *mahua* flowers, mango and wild grasses for self consumption or for selling them to forest Contractors or co-operative societies. The privileges and concessions were few and uneconomical in comparison with their past free access to the forests. Nqdi of Rakaiya complained "our fore-fathers planted fruit trees in the forests. Those trees still bloom and bear fruits. We see that our trees are there but we cannot touch them because they are in the *jarah jungle* (Reserved Forests) which once belonged to us". The prohibition on hunting of big games dried up an important source of Korwa food supply. Smaller games like *Kotri* and *Kharha* were extensively killed not by the Hill Korwa only but by other neighbouring tribes also. The traders erticed the tribals, especially the Hill Korwa to kill deer and barter its meat with equal weight of rice. As a result of intensive killing now the forests of Surgjua and Raigarh are almost devoid of smaller species of animals. Reservation of forests and the various restrictions accompanying it have curtailed the freedom of movement of Korwas in forests. Thus, the forest dwelling tribe has been reduced to the status of hired labourers. Under the present circumstances the Hill Korwa cannot hunt freely. There are restrictions on collection of certain forest products and the grazing rights have been curtailed to such an extent that the cattle must be confined within the demarcated areas. The Hill Korwa feel the pinch of these restrictions at every stage of their economic life.

The game laws, as said ealier have deprived the Hill Korwa of his meat dish which was a substantial factor in providing him some protein food. Whatever little meat he is able to collect by way of hunting small games, he does so with a sense of guilt and perpetual fear, lest he is punished for his illegal activities.

Strict forest regulations have deprived the Hill Korwa from hunting and food gathering to a considerable extent and have made them dependent on *grihats* in search of cash money even for primary needs. As a result of their contact with the alien patterns of living, the Hill Korwa have acquired a taste for new items of consumption which are readily supplied by the *grihats* on loan.

Forests are resources of national wealth and they must be protected with all measures at our command but not at the cost of forest dwelling tribes whose entire existence is based on forests. The forest products are exploited and exported in order to enhance the national revenue. As a result of this policy, the forest dwelling tribes face extinction and the Government in order to protect and develop the tribals spends huge amount of money without ushering any significant break-through in this respect. It the forest dwellers are given the first priority on the collection of forest products, this may compensate the loss that the people had to suffer due to changing forest laws.

Development of Transport and Communication

Opening up of the interior tracts to the world outsiue is the biggest single factor responsible for bringing about change in the Korwa economy. The Ambikapur-Ranchi road exposed the main Korwa belt of Shankargarh, Jonkapath, Sanna and Khudia to the outsiders. The Batoli-Kamleshwarpur road passes through Korwa settlements of Main path. Bansajhal and Sardapath also are well connected through Batoli-Bagicha road and Begicha-Sardapath road. Rakaiya in Surguja is situated about 4 Kms from the old Ambikapur Ranchi road. Bansajhal is situated about 2 Kms off Batoli-Bagicha Road. Maltipur and Sardapath are situated on main roads.

Development of transport during the last fifty years has been mainly responsible for development of Shankargarh Batoli and Bagicha markets where traders from Haryana and Rajasthan have also established their shops. These market centres cater to the needs of the Hill Korwa of Jonkapath, Mainpath, Surguja, Sardapath, and Gaiburapath (Raigarh District). These roads have facilitated the movements of itinerant traders and vendors selling clothes, blankets, salt, spices, and cheap ornaments. Most of these traders come from Palamu District of adjoining Bihar state. In course of time these traders settled down near Korwa settlements, purchased tribal lands, and became *grihats.* The tracts of land which once belonged to the Hill Korwa reached in the hands of the traders-cum-petty land owners. Alienated from lands the Hill Korwa accepted a subordinate position under the *grihats.* The *Sahukars* subsequently established close commercial links with the *grihats* in order to extract tribal commodities and export them out to the regional market.

The *grihat*, therefore, advances loans in cash or in the form of food grains to the Hill Korwa and insist that the payment should be made in the form of oil-seeds. Thus the

Hill Korwa are forced to cultivate oilseeds instead of millets which is their staple diet. It is, therefore, important to note that the Korwa cannot grow what they want to for their consumption and instead grow according to the demand of *Sahukars* and the market. The commercialisation of the Korwa crops seems to be a direct result of improvement of transport facilities which, on the other hand, led to the development of market economy.

Development in transport net-work exposed the Hill Korwa to alien cultural patterns and value systems. Last few decades showed a remarkable change in material culture of the Hill Korwa. The traditional "scare-crow" appearence of Hill korwa with bows and arrows dangling with the coiffer and shining bare bodies with a strip of cloth to cover the private parts exists no more. Instead these people purchase ready made shirts and blouses from the local markets. A few keep umbrellas, torches, and plastic combs. Hitherto unknown spices now season the Krowa dishes. Aluminium and brass-were have replaced and earthern ware. The Chamars, in old days, used to supply foot-wear to the Hill Korwa free of cost in return corpse of cattle. Now the politico-economic elite of the tribe purchase the same from the *grihats*. Very few people belonging to the last generation of the tribe ever visited Ambikapur but now they travel frequently to the district and tehsil headquarters by buses which ply regularly in fair-weather. Gradually the Hill Korwa are looking forward beyond the village ambit for fulfilment of their economic needs through cash money which comes by sale of property, borrowing, and labour. Money is the medium of exchange instead of the age old system of barter which now exists only sparsely. The ideas of saving and investment of money for its further growth as a result of contact with other cultures have also been picked up by a few members of the tribe. Mahuari of Rakaiya, who has mortgaged her lands to the covillagers and has invested money in the form of small loans may be taken as an example. The change of the Korwa economy from self-snfficiency to the total dependence on money and market seems to be the direct result of development of transport net-work in the area.

Opening of liquor shops

The traditional drinks of the Hill Korwa are *handi* and *jagra*. The former is prepared from millets or rice whereas the latter by brewing *mahua* flowers. *Jagra* is seasonal drink and is consumed rarely but *handi* is the most popular beverage which is inseparable form almost all the life-cycle rituals of the people. Though its real nutritive value cannot be ascertained at present, nevertheless, the people consider it not only a drink but as a full meal.

Under the present excise laws, the authorised contractors have the legal rights to manufacture and sell country made liquor (*daru*) within a specified area. These distilleries are fast replacing the traditional *handi* because of easy availability of distilled liquor. The influence of liquor is stronger and longer lasting than the *handi*. Easy availability of *daru* at the thresholds of each Hill Korwa household has been made possible by opening of illegal *gaddis* in Korwa villages. As already stated, the *gaddis* are usually given to the Hill Korwa on commission basis which is paid in the form of liquor. This shrewed technique of the contractors trap many unwilling drinkers.

The contracts for manufacturing and sale of liquor are auctioned on yearly basis. The successful bidders run their establishment with a view to earning maximum profit in the minimum period of time. They, therefore encourage drinking among the tribals by distributing liquor free of cost on the day of opening of a new distillery and on the last day of contract. The unwilling drinkers are sometimes harassed and belaboured on some pretext or the other by the owners of liquor shops. The houses of unwilling Korwa drinkers are raided by the hirelings of the contractors. A hill Korwa cannot stand so much pressure, harassment, and hardship. He, therefore, indulges in drinking partly due to his inherent weakness for liquor and partly due to fear of reprisals.

The liquor is made available to a Hill Korwa on loan. If this loan is not paid within the stipulated time limit, the same is automatically converted into money for which exorbitant rate of interest is charged. The minimum rate of interest prevalent in the tribal areas of Chattisgarh is 50 per cent per annum. If a Hill Korwa takes a drink in return of millets suffers a loss to the tune of 150 per cent.

The habit of increasing liquor addietion has influenced the Korwa life both collectively and individually, The impact of alcoholism on the society has been discussed by the present author somewhere else in details[2]. Here the impact of liquor shops on the society and economy will be discussed briefly.

The Hill Korwa grew millets in *bewar* fields and collected *mahua* flowers from the forests. They were capable of preparing *renu jari* a concoction used for fermenting millets or *mahua* flowers for preparation of *handi* and *jagra* respectively. The *handi* and *jagra* were prepared on selected occasion by private individuals. On any such occasions all the villagers and members of the host kindred living in other villages were invited to enjoy the homemade drink. It served as a medium through which an individual could raise his socio-economic prestige. On the other hand, individuals committing an offence against the society were liable to punishment in the form of ostracization and their reunion with the society was possible only through the acceptance of *handi* by the society on behalf of the erring individual. In case of purification from pollution through bereavement, the same procedure is adopted. Hence preparation of *Handi* always signified an important occasion for the person who prepared it for the kinsmen who consumed it.

Yields of millets had gone down after abolition of shifting cultivation and the quantity of *Handi* manufactured and consumed also started shrinking. The opening of liquor shops came as a deterrent to the manufacture of *handi*, and the Hill Korwa felt attracted towards liquor shops.

In the traditional system of drinking, money was not involved as a medium of exchange and the tribe was self sufficent in manufacturing *handi* Opening of liquor shops made money as the medium of exchange. A Hill Korwa, in search of money to pay for his drinks sold out his land, his household articles, the happiness of his married life and even his honour.

As already stated, the Red Turban Chief[3] of Rakaiya mortgaged his turban for a bottle of *daru* to the owner of liquor shop. The Red turban is given to a regional Korwa Chief, a position, considered to be the most coveted among the Hill Korwa.

The present Korwa Chief or Diwan is said tb have lost all his ancestral property due to his drinking habits; even now, he passes most of his time at the village liquor shop.

Bodhna of Maltipur was divorced twice by his subsequent wives as he mortgaged not only his scanty belonging but even his bows and arrows. He was unfit and unable to afford his subsequent wives.

Koka Korwa of Rakaiya was alleged to have killed his mother under influence of liquor, as the latter refused to give him money for drinking. Her murder was avenged by the members of her clan by killing Koka. Koka' s brothers took revenge and caused serious injuries to many a villager. Thus, Koka's demand for money to purchase liquor led to his own and his mother's murder and unleashed an unending cycle of atrocities involving further hardships.

The failure in rehabilitating the Hill Korwa into settled villages may be attributed mainly to their addiction to liquor and restriction on brewing of home-made beer. Purchase of liquor required money and money was procured through selling land, cattle, and other belongings.

Hence the opening of liquor shops not only broke the tribal self, sufficiency in manufacturing drinks but made them dependent on money for purchase of distilled liquor.

REFERENCES

1. Nag, D.S. ibid 5.
2. Rizvi, B.R. 1971. "The Hill Korwa and Alcoholism : A case study" in Tribe, VII(4), 33-37.
3. — 1977. "Political Organization of the Hill Korwa of Surguja (M.P.)" in *Chattisgarh : An Area Study*, Edited by Dr. A.K. Danda, Calcutta, Anthropological Survey of India.

CHAPTER SEVEN

The Hill Korwa at Cross Roads: Suggestions and Prospects

The changing society and economy of the Hill Korwa of Chattisgarh since the abolition of *beora* in 1867 have been discussed in the preceding chapter, It has been described how an economically self-sufficient group of shifting cultivators was forced by circumstances to adopt plough-cultivation. Now the tribe is standing at the threshold of joining the teeming millions of India's labour force which ekes out their livelihood through utter dependence on a system which is purely based on monetary and market economy. How did the tribe reach to such a pass ? How best can this crisis be averted ? What were or are the basic flaws in planning for the development of the tribe ? How best the group can be exposed to the forces of "cumulative development" leading to modernization ? Some of these questions may be reviewed here.

Fallacious Planning

The Hill Korwa were evicted from the forests with a view to conserving forests for maintenance of ecological balance and preservation of national wealth. The effort seemed commendable at its outset but proved to be disastrous as the decades passed by. The planner uprooted a forest tribe from their age old habitat and appointed forest contractors belonging to an alien culture. These inducted new-comers had no sense of sympathy and belongingness to the forests. As a result illicit forest felling continued unabated. The Hill Korwa, on the other hand, had their ancestral spirits and deities either on a forest tree or beneath it. Their ancestors planted scores of fruit bearing trees which were never felled as a matter of principle even during *beora* cultivation. The alien contractors had no such impediments. They denuded forests more speedily than generations of the Hill Korwa could think of.

The Hill Korwa were evicted from their forest abode with a view to conserving national wealth. It appears as of the Hill Korwa were not considered as beneficiaries of national wealth. Only the industries were considered as the beneficiaries of forest wealth which add further to national wealth. It is an irony of the situation that the valuable national wealth which was derived from uprooting people from their natural habitat was again spent on the welfare of the same uprooted people in the form of giving them ready-made houses, lands, draught cattle, and seeds.

The uprooted mass of tribals never felt happy with the newly provided houses situated far away from their traditional abode. They deserted them surreptiously. The land and bullocks were sold off. The agencies of welfare put the entire blame on the people who did not want to change, and who are, now, an incorrigible lot. This vicious cycle must be broken at some stage. The officials of the forest department should behave and work as an intimate friend and guide of their fellow human beings instead of playing the role of a forest police.

Formal Economic Models and Non-market or Peripheral Market Societies

The Hill Korwa, who have moved in the last few decades, from a non-market society to peripheral-market society are the major victims of a planning which was initially based on a formal economic proposition that in-put materials are relatively proportional to out-put. The people were given lands, draught cattle and seeds with the hope that the Hill Korwa by adopting settled agriculture will ultimately become prosperous. Events went contrary to the planner's hopes and aspirations. Little the planner thought that the economy of a forest tribe is embedded in the forest only. The people had no sense of belongingness to land. Danda reports: "With the abolition of shifting cultivation......the Kodaku have returned to food-gathering from food producing economy......The Nagesia is the only tribe......who could make a smooth change over from settled to permanent settled cultivation. Even now the members of this tribe take recourse to their old practice when such opportunities are available[3]".

It is apparent from the above statement that with the sole exception of a part of Nagesia tribe, none of the forest tribe of Chattisgarh have adopted to settled cultivation successfully. The failure shown by the Hill Korwa in adopting settled agriculture may be attributed to their indifferent attitude towards land.

The Indian peasantry in general treats land as an embodiment of a benevolent female deity, the reverent mother. This assumption preoccupied the minds of the planners who thought that by giving land, seeds, and cattle, the HIll Korwa could be made successful settled agriculturists. The Korwa mythology and folklore does not contain even a scant reference to land as a benevolent deity. The Hill Korwa are not alone in not having a reverent attitude towards earth. The impoverished southern Italians, the Andalusean and the fellahin of Arabia work for themselves and not for the land, they do not feel that land is the extension of themselves.

It was presumed by the agencies responsible for development of the Hill Korwa that adoption of settled agriculture probably contained the only solution to eradicate poverty from the Hill Korwa.

"Poverty", says Dalton[4], "mean not only insufficient food but also eradicable disease, early death, and a life sentence of ignorance, immobility and meanness". The Hill Korwa are the real poor as nothing has so far been done to provide them medical assistance, education, and employment. Gunner

Myrdal has said rightly that "development must be understood as movement upwards of the entire social system".

Socially the Hill Korwa occupy the lowest rung of hierarchical ladder of the tribal peasantry of Chattisgarh. Yet no educational facilities were available to the Hill Korwa. Wherever such facilities were available, either schools were managed by the high caste Hindus or they were situated far from Korwa settlements where small children could not reach. Medical hospitals were situated 10 to 12 kilometres away from the village inhabited by the Hill Korwa. Hence, patients, even in the dire need of medical assistance were forced to be left at the mercy of the *baigas* (priests) and *dewars* (diviners). It will be erroneous to assume that the Hill Korwa are not receptive to modern educational and medical facilities. Wherever such opportunities are available, they derive maximum benefit from them.

Once the idea of making the Hill Korwa settled agriculturists came to the planners' mind, it was left on the Hill Korwa to become expert agriculturists. No demonstration plots were organised near the Korwa hamlets. None of the Korwa villages visited by the author had an irrigation or drinking water well. The Hill Korwa were not told how best the rocky lands with a thin layer of soil could be exploited fruitfully. None was told about the improved and high yielding seeds. They were completely unaware of the utility of chemical fertilizers. In short, the Hill Korwa benefited minimum from all developmental activities in Chattisgarh. The Village Level Workers always lived away from the hamlets where the Hill Korwa lived. The Korwa villages were least visited by the government officials.

Opening of licensed liquor shops and breweries has replaced the practice of drinking traditional home-made beer. The liquor has not only brought about the forces of exploitation on the surface but has ruined the Korwa economy. Here again, one can notice the same vicious circle in operation. The government is spending huge sums on tribal development on the one hand and the tribals on the other hand are squandering their money on liquor. Neither the government nor the tribals gain anything from the existing excise policies. The people who really gain are the middlemen who exploit the tribals on one hand and always try to by-pass the legal provisions protecting the tribals. A spurt of unauthorised *gaddis* in the tribal villages of Chattisgarh have removed all restrictions from the movement and distribution of liquor. It is flooding tribal villages with liquor.

Addiction to liquor is not only a social problem but it has put a tremendous strain on the already bad economy of tribe. The people try to satisfy their urge by stealing, or begging or borrwoing. This has earned a bad name to a brave people.

It is therefore recommended to ban all unauthorised *gaddis* and observance of frequent "dry days" for weaning away the tribals from liquor. The traditional form of brewing should be encouraged and all restrictions imposed on it should be immediately removed. This may provide a fillip to the tardy agricultural production. The licensed liquor shops should be phased out gradually. There seems to be some substance when Elwin says, "If I had my way I would close licensed liquor shops and would have a social branch of Community Development Ministry to teach the brewing of beer.[6]" I wish Elwin would have had his way.

Having alienated from land and cattle, a growing number of Hill Korwa are resorting to serfdom of the local *grihats*, who have been cunningly exploiting all resources of the Hill Korwa. What the latter get as a pittance is a handful of food grains and heaps of insults, humiliation, and abuses. Hours of work and other service conditions are undefined depending largely on the sweet will of a *grihat*. There is a need to save the Hill Korwa from the clutches of the cruel landlords. Government should frame legislation to provide some protection to the tribals. The hours of work, the wages and other service conditions should be specifically defined and the provisions of the law should be strictly implemented. While discouraging bonded labour, new employment avenues must be created for the tribals lest they are confronted with a more serious economic catastrophy since abolition of *beora*.

There is a clamour for new primary schools in Korwa villages. In the existing primary schools high caste Hindu teachers do not usually stay long partly due to their domestic problems and partly due to fear of pollution. It is, therefore, suggested that all the schools situated in Korwa villages should preferably be managed by the Korwa teachers only. If sufficient number of Korwa teachers is not available, teachers from other tribes should be given preference to work in Korwa villages. In case, tribal teachers are also not available, the task should be assigned to low caste teachers.

Once it has been decided that the Hill Korwa would be made settled agriculturist, lands should be distributed once more to the landless and henceforth the tribal lands must not be allowed to change hand either through mortgage or dispose. Banking facilities should be extended to the tribal areas and a close liaison should be established between the tribals and bank personnel so that the latter get themselves appraised of tribal needs. Each bank should adopt atleast one tribe in Chattisgarh instead of a village which, in most of the cases, is multi-ethnic. The real benefit in such villages reaches only to its upper elites. If a tribe is adopted all its segments will probably be benefited. By adoption, here, we mean that the selected tribes should be provided maximum borrowing facilities depending upon repaying capacity of individuals. Short term loans should be provided to the Hill Korwa for contingencies like procurement of agricultural inputs. The rates of interest should be differential according to socio-economic status of a tribe. Specific criteria and occasions should be fixed for grant of loans.

Many areas in Surguja and Raigarh district remain cut off five months in a year during rainy seasons. For this period all developmental activities come to a standstill. Government officials feel themselves completely isoltaed there. Educational and medical facilities in such areas are almost non-existent. Hence the government officials feel extremely concerned about the fate of their children who cannot get proper education or treatment. Lack of medical facilities forces them to visit district headquarters frequently.

Due to non-availability of transport during rainy seasons the officials on duty face tremendous difficulties in moving from one place to another. These cumulative problems unnerve them and they try to get out of difficult places before the onset of rains. If a public servant fails to do so he gives full vent to his vengeance against the local inhabitants for whom he is supposed to work. Consequently, not only the aboriginals suffer but the processes of development also come to a stand-still position.

Hence, for a speedy implementation of development schemes, government should be considerate to the problems of its employees. People working in difficult and remote places deserve more incentives in terms of quick promotions, additional increments, and certificates of merit. A time limit should be fixed for the personnel working in such areas. Requests for transfer from respective officials should be entertained only after expiry of the stipulated time limit.

The above suggestions do not present a solution for all the problems faced by the Hill Korwa. Administrators, welfare agencies, and non-tribal neighbours will have to go a long way to understand the real problems of the people and seek their solutions. Nevertheless, the Hill Korwa need a special deal. They need more sympathy and understanding from those who are living in their neighbourhood and those who are responsible for their welfare. The Hill Korwa should be protected from the clutches of exploiters who take undue advantage of the latter's sickening ignorance and utter simplicity. The government should assume the sole responsibility of protecting the Hill Korwa from the octopus of exploitation whose tentacles are *grihats*, *Sahukars*, petty officials, ignorance, disease, penury, fatalism, and total resignation to the interest in life.

REFERENCES

1. Bohannan, P. and G. Dalton. 1962. 'Introduction' in *Markets in Africa*, North Western University: 2.

2.	Danda, A.K.		ibid, 61.
3.	Redfield, Robert.	1961.	"Peasant view of Good Life" in *Peasant Society and Cultures*, Chicago, University Press: 60-88.
4.	Dalton, G.	1971.	*Economic Anthropology and Development*, New York, Basic Books, Inc. : 271.
5.	Myrdal, Gunner.	1975.	"The Unity in Social Sciences" in *Human Organisation*, 34 (4) : 328.
6.	Elwin, Verrier.	1964.	*The Tribal World of Verrier Elwin*, Bombay, Oxford University Press: 335.

Appendix

APPENDIX I

Korwa Kinship Terms

Relationship	Term of address	Term of reference	Remarks
NUCLEAR FAMILY			
Wife (W)	—	Aimin	Teknonymy
Husband (H)	—	Loga, ghar muar	Teknonymy
Mother (M)	Aya	Aya	
Elder son (eS)	Babu	Barka, by name	
Younger son (YS)	Nuding	babu, Chotka, by name	
Elder Brother (eB)	Dada	Dada	
Younger Brother (yB)	Babu	Babu, by nameon Child's name	
Elder Sister (eZ)	Didi	Didi	
Younger Sister (YZ)	Nonee	Nonee, by name	
Father (F)	Dau, babu Apan		

Relationship	Term of address	Term of reference	Remarks
JOINT FAMILY			
SS	Nati	Korian	
SW	Bahuria	Kimini	
SD	Natini	Korain	
F.F.	Aja	Aja	
FeB	Bara	Gungoo	
FeBW	Bari	Gungoo	
FeBS	Dada	Dada	
FBeD	Didi	Didi	
FBYD	Nonee	by name	
FYB	Kaka	Pitya Kaka	
FZ	Mami	Mamo	
eBW	Hilly	Hilly	
FYBW	Kaki	Kaki	
YBW	—	Leinkoo	Avoidance
YBS	Bara	Gungoo	
YBD	Bari	Gungoo	
HF	Dau	Sosur	
HM	Aice	Sais	
HeB	—	Bhasur	Avoidance
HeZ	Didi	Derh sais	
HYZ	Nooni by name	Nanand	
HYB	Babu by name	Deur, Deura	Joking
AGNATES			
F.F.F.	Bara	Gungu	
F.F.M.	Bari	,,	
SSS	Bara	,,	
SSSD	Bari	,,	
FFZ	Aji	Aji	
BSS	Nati	Karain	
BSD	Natini	,,	
FFB	Aja	Aju	
FFBW	Aji	Aji	

Relationship	Term of address	Term of reference	Remarks
FFBZ	Bari	Gungoo	
FFBD	Mami	Mami	
HBSS	Nati	Korain	
HBSeD	Didi	Derh sais	
HFBeS	—	Bhasur	Avoidance
FATHER'S SISTER'S HUSBAND			
FZH	Mama	Mama	
HFZH	Mama	Mama-Sasur	
WFZH	Mama	Mama-Sasur	
WBSW	Bahuria	Kimini	
FSeS	Sasur	Derh-Sasur	
FSYS	Babu	Sara	
FZeD	—	Derh sais	Avoidance
F.S.YD	Mooni	Sari	Joking
SISTER'S HUSBAND			
eZH	Bhato	Tiyan	
YZH	Arain	Bahin damad	
ZHeB	Mama	Mama	
ZHYB	by name	Sara	
ZHEZ	+	Derh sais	Avoidance
ZHYZ	by name	Sari	Joking
ZS	Bhegna	Bhancha	
ZD	Bhegni	Bhanchi	
ZSW	Behuria	Bhanchi	
ZHF	Mama	Mama	
ZDH	Damad	Damad	
ZHM	Mami	Mami	
HeZH	Derh-Sasur	Arain	Avoidance
HYZH	Damad		
HZS	Bhegna	Bhancha	
HZD	Bhegni	Bhanchi	
DAUGHTER'S HUSBAND			
DH	Damad	Arain	
DZ	Natin	Korain	

Relationship	Term of address	Term of reference	Remarks
DD	Natini	Korain	
DHB	Bhegua	Bhancha	
DHBW	Bhegni	Bhanchi	
DHF	Samdhi	Samdhi	
DHM	—	Samdhin	
DSW	Natini	Korain	
DDH	Nati	Korain	
MOTHER			
MB	Mama	Mama	
MBW	Mami	Mami	
MeZ	Bari	Gungoo	
MYZ	Kaki	Kaki	
MF	Aja	Aja	
M.M.	Aji	Aji	
MBD	+	+	
MBeS	Sara Samdhi	Samdhi	
MBYS	Sara babu	Saura	
HMB	Mamue	Mama-Sasur	
HMBW	Mami	Mami-Sais	
HMF	Aja	Aja	
HMM	Aji	Aji	
HMZ	Sais	Sais	
WIFE			
W.eB	Derh-sasur	Sasur	
WYB	Babu, father of 'so and so'	Sara	
WEZ	+	Derh-sais	Avoidance
WYZ	Nooni	Sari	Joking
WF	Mama	Sasur	
WM	Mami	Sais	
WFZ	Mami	Mami-sais	
WMZ			
WFF	Aja	Aja	
WFM	Aji	Aji	

Relationship	Term of address	Term of reference	Remarks
WeBW	+	Lainkoo Bharrah	Avoidance
WZH	Sadhu	Sadhu	
WBS	Bhegua	Bhancha	
WBD	Bhegni	Bhanchu	
WZS	Bara	Gungoo	
WZD	Bari	Gungoo	
Son's wife			
SWF	Samdhi	Samdhi	
SWM	+	Samdhi	
SWS	Bahuria	Bhanchi	
SWB	Bhegna	Bhancha	
SWBW	Bhegni	Bhanchi	
SWZH	damad	Bhancha	

APPENDIX—II

Agricultural Calendar

Sl. No.	Name of local month	English Equivalent	Type of soil	Crops	Agricultural operations
1	2	3	4	5	6
1.	Magh	January-February	Danr	Oil-seed (mustard-Jantgi)	Harvesting and threshing
2.	Phagun	February-March	Danr	Millet (Gondli)	Ploughing and leveling of field
				Ropa Paddy	-do-
3.	Chait	March-April	Danr	Millet (Gondli)	Ploughing, leveiling and manuring
				Ropa Paddy	-do-
4.	Baisakh	April-May	Danr	Millet (Gondli)	Ploughing
				Madia, Serali	-do-
				Maize	-do-
				Paddy	-do-
				Pulses (Rahar)	-do-
5.	Jeth	May-June	Danr	Gondli	Ploughing
				Gora Paddy	-do-

1	2	3	4	5	6
6.	Asaadh	June-July	Danr	Millets-Gondli	Sowing
				Madia	Sowing
				Serali	Sowing
				Minjhri	Sowing
				Maize	Sowing
				Pulses (Rahar)	
7.	Sawan	July-August			
8.	Bhadon	August-September	Danr	Pulses (Kurthi)	Ploughing
				Oilseed (Jantgi)	Ploughing & Sowing
				Millets (Minjhri)	Harvesting
9.	Kuar	September-October	Danr	Paddy	Harvesting
				Oilseed (Jantgi)	Sowing
				Pulses (Kurthi)	Sowing
				Millets (Minjhri)	Harvesting
				Maize	Harvesting
10.	Kartik	October-November	Danr	Oilseeds (Mustard)	Ploughing & Sowing
				Pulses (Kurthi)	Harvesting
				Millets (Minjhri)	Harvesting
				Maize	Harvesting

1		2	3	4	5
11.	Aghan	November-December	Danr	Pulses (Kurthi)	Threshing
				Millets (Minjhri, Serali)	Harvesting & Threshing, Harvesting
				Maize	Harvesting
12.	Pous	December-January	Danr	Pulses (Rahar)	Harvesting, Threshing
				Oilseeds (Jantgi)	-do-
				Mustard	-do-

APPENDIX—III

List of Villages Visited by the Author

District : Surguja (M.P.)

Tehsil : Bamripath

1. Amgaon
2. Barpain
3. Biria (Jaswantpur)
4. Chirai
5. Doomarpath (Durgapur)
6. Hargawan
7. Hutook Danr
8. Indakond
9. Jampani
10. Jonkapath
11. Kanjia
12. Katari Kona
13. Khar Kona
14. Kotli
15. Laladara
16. Mahuadari
17. Parewa
18. Patna
19. Patratoli (Jarha Dih)
20. Rakaiya
21. Tangartoli
22. Tendupara (Jagma)
23. Vinayakpur

Tehsil : Ambikapur

1. Ambapani

2. Bansajhal
3. Gobindpur
4. Kardana
5. Karwan
6. Khoontapani (Tirang)
7. Maduasarai
8. Maltipur
9. Moosakhor
10. Surdragadhari

District : Raigarh (M.P.)

Tehsil : Jashpur

1. Durgapur
2. Gaiburapath
3. Kerapath
4. Maini
5. Samarbar
6. Sardapath.

Note : Places shown in parenthesis denote village names against which hamlet names are mentioned.

Bibliography

1. Allami, Abul Fazl. 1596. *Ain-e-Akbari* (Tr) H. Blochmann, Delhi, 129.
2. Ahmad, S.H. 1973. "Anthropometric measurements of the Korwa of Surguja", *Eastern Anthropologist*. 16 (2) : 79-106.
3. Allee, E.M. 1949. *Principles of Animal Ecology*, Philadelphia : W.B. Saunders : 1
4. Apte, J.S. 1960. "Co-operative movement among the Tribes of District Thana, Bombay State", *Vanyajati*, VIII (3): 102-104.
5. Bailey, F.G. 1969. "Capital, Saving and Credit in Highland Orissa (India)" in *Capital* Saving *and Credit in Peasant Societies*, Edited by Raymond Firth and B.S.Yamey, London, George Allen and Unwin : 104-132.
6. Barnet, H.G. 1968. "Making Money", in *Economic Anthropology : Reading in Theory and Analysis*. Edited by Edward E. Leclair and Harold K. Schneider : New York, Holt Rinehart
7. Bennett, John W. 1968. "Reciprocal Economic Exchange among the North American Agricultural Operators" *South Western Journal of Anthropology*, 24 (3) : 276-309.

8. Bhaduri, M.B. 1937 "The Korwa of Udaipur State" in *Man in India,* 17 : 127-46.

9. Bhandari, J.S. 1963. "Kinship, Family and Marriage among the Korwas of Dudhi", *Eastern Anthropologist,* 16 (2) : 79-106.

10. Bohannan, and G. Dalton. 1962. 'Introduction' in *Markets in Africa* North Western University : 2.

11. Chattopadhyaya, K.P. 1947. "Economic conditions of the Kurkus of Melghat Forest", *Journal of Royal Asiatic Society of Bengal.* XII (1) :

12. Cook, Scott. 1966. "The obsolete antimarket mentality ; A critique to Economic Anthropology", *American Anthropologist,* 68 (1) : 323-345.

13. Crooks, W. 1892. "A vocabulary of Korwa language *Journal of Asiatic Society of Bengal.* LXI, I : 125.

14. Dalton, E.T. 1872. *Descriptive Ethnology of Bengal,* Calcutta, Mukhopadhyaya : 220-228.

15. Dalton, G. 1969. "Theoretical issues in Economic Anthropology", *Current Anthropology,* 10 (1) : 63-102.

16. ——— 1971. *Economic Anthropology and Development,* New York. Basic Books Inc. : 271.

17. Danda, A.K. 1977. "Tribal Economy in Chattisgarh" in *Chattisgarh : An area study,* Edited by A.K. Danda, Calcutta, pp. 92-119. Anthropological Survey of India.

18. ——— 1977. "Tribal Situation in North East Surguja" in *Tribal Situation in North East Surguja,* Calcutta, Anthropological Survey of India : 4.

19. Danda, A.K. et al. 1977. Economic Life in a Korwa Village in *Tribal Situation in North East Surguja*, Edited by A.K. Danda, Calcutta, Anthropological Survey of India : 116.

20. de Brett, E. A, 1909. *Chattisgarh Feudatory Gazetteer*, Bombay : 233-236.

21. District Census Handbook 1964. Surguja District, Census of India 1961.

22. ——— 1964. Raigarh District, Census of India 1961.

23. Driver, W.H.P. 1891. "Notes on some Kolarian Tribes in *Journal of Royal Asiatic Society ofBengal*. Vol. LX (Part I) : 24

24. Dube, S.C. 1947. "The Economic Life of Kamar", *Man in India*, XXVI (2): 137-169.

25. Dutta, Majumdar. 1940. "The Economic Organization of Bhotia" (Report).

26. Elwin, Verrier. 1964. *The Tribal World of Verrier Elwin*, Bombay ; Oxford University Press : 335.

27. Epstein, Scarlett 1967. "Productive efficiency and customary systems of rewards in rural South India" in *Themes in Economic Anthropology*. Edited by Raymond Firth, London, Tavistock : 229-252.

28. Firth, Raymond 1951. *The Elements of Social Organisation*, London, C.A. Watts.

29. ——— 1969. "Capital, Saving and Credit in Peasant Societies—A view point from Economic Anthropology" in *Capital, Saving and Credit in Peasant Societies*, Edited by Raymond Firth and B.S. Yamey London, George Allen and Unwin : 18.

30. Grierson, G.A. 1967. *Linguistic Survey of India*. IV, 147-151.

31. Haimendorf, Von-Furer. 1949. "Seasonal Nomadism and Economics of Chenchus of Hyderabad" in *Journal of Royal Asiatic Society of Bengal*, VI : 175-196.

32. Herskovits, M.J. 1952. *Economic Anthropology*, New York : Alfred and Knopf: 88.

33. Hussain, Syed Khaya Mehaboob 1949. "The Rural uplift of Tribes and Backward Classes in Hyderabad Deccan" in *Man in India*. XXIX (3) and (4) 185-198.

34. Hutton, J.H. 1946. *Caste in India* (Glossary), London, Oxford Universty Press : 80.

35. Kaplan David. 1968. "The Formal-substantive controversy in Economic Anthropology : Reflections on its wider implications", *South-western Journal of Anthropology*, 24 (3) : 228-251.

36. Karve, Iravati. 1953. *Kinship Organisation of India* Poona, Deccan College : 284-289.

37. Leclair Edward, E. Jr. 1962. "Economic Theory and Economic Anthropology", *American Anthropologist*, 64 : 1179-1203.

38. Lewis, Arthur W. 1962. "Foreword" in *Economic Development and Social Change in South India* by Scarlett Epstein Manchester, Manchester Univesity Press.

39. Majumdar, D.N. 19?0. "The Economic Background of Social Institutions in Primitive Societies", *Man in India*, 10 (2 and 3) : 10-66.

40.	——	1944.	*Fortunes of Primitive Tribes*, Lucknow, Universal Publishers Limited.
41.	Marshal	1936.	*Principles of Economics*, London : 150-166.
42.	Mukherjee, B.	1955.	'Riang Economy' in *Bulletin*, Anthropological Survey of India, XIV (2).
43.	Mukherjee, Ram Krishna.	1962.	"On classification of Family Structures in *Indian Anthropology*, Edited by T.N. Madan and Gopala Saran, New Delhi Asia Publishing House : 352-398.
44.	Murdock, G.P.	1969.	*Social Structure*, New York, Mac Millan : 223-224.
45.	Myrdal, Gunnar.	1975.	"The Unity of Social Sciences" in *Human Organisation* 34 (4): 328.
46.	Nag, D.S.	1958.	*Tribal Economy*, Delhi, Bharatiya Adimjati Sevak Sangh 120.
47.	Nash, Manning.	1961.	"The Social context of Economic choice in a small society", *Man* LXI : 186-191
48.	Notes and Queries in Anthropology	1960.	London, Routledge and Keggan Paul : 221.
49.	Panoff Michel.	1970.	"Marcel Mauss's the Gift Revisited", *Man*, Vol. 5 (1) : 60-70.
50.	Prasad, Narmadeshwar	1961.	"Korwa" in *Land and People of Tribal Bihar*, Ranchi, 193-196,
51.	Polanyi, Karl.	1957.	"The Economy as Instituted Process" in *Trade and Market in the early Empires*, Glencoe, Illinois, The Free Press : 243-270.

52. Redfield, Robert. 1961. Peasant view of Good Life in *Peasant Society and Culture,* Chicago, University Press : 60-88.

53. Report of Commission for Scheduled Castes and Scheduled Tribes for 1968-1969 and 1970-1971.

54. Risley, H.H. and E.P. Gail 1901. Census of India, Vol. 1, Part I, Report : 415.

55. Rizvi, B.R. 1971. "The Korwa and Alcoholism A case study', *Tribe,* VII (4) : 33-37.

56. ——— 1977. Political Organization of the Hill Korwa of Surguja (M.P.) in *Chattisgarh : An area study,* Edited by A.K. Danda, {Calcutta, Anthropological Survey of India.

57. Roy, S.C. 1915. *The Oraon of Chota Nagpur,* Ranchi.

58. Russel, R.V. and R.B. Hiralal. 1916. *The Tribes and Castes of Central India,* IV, London. Macmillan.

59. Samuelson, Paul, A. 1964. *Economics : An Introductory Analysis.* New York, Mc Grew Hill.

60. Sandhwar. 1973. "The method of Christian conversion among the Tribes The Korwa converts of Palamu ; a case study", *Journal of Social Research,* 1.

61. Singhdeo, S.B. 1957. *Surguja ka ek Adhayayan,* Ambikapur : 22-24 and 181-226.

Glossary of Local Terms

A

Adha Batai	A form of share cropping
Agua	Mediator of a marriage negotiations
Amba	Mango (*Maugifera indical*)
Amli	Tamarind (*Tamarindus indica*)
Ason	*Terminalia tomentoea*
Awla	*Phyllanthus melacocylon*

B

Balga	Priest
Baint	Handle
Bakas	Land in the cultivating possession of land-lord
Balua	Axe
Bandha	Mortgage
Bar	Bride-groom
Beetha hudoo	Paddy sown by broadcasting method
Bel	A roundish fruit
Beonra/bewar	Swidden cultivation
Ber	Prunus domestica
Bhaiyar	A lineage group member of which trace their descent from a single common male ancestor.
Bhathi	Brewery-cum-shop
Bhaunri	A form of marriage dance around the *madua*

Bhitar-deo	A household deity whose shrine is situated inside the interior room.
Bhitar-ghar	The room which serves as a shrine to Bhitar-deo
Biri	Indigenous cigar
Biyari	Sun-set meals
Bura Bandha	orm of Admortgage

C

CARE	Council for American Relief Everywhere
Char	Buchanania latifolia
Chela	A disciple ef the diviner (*dewar*)
Cherta	A post-harvest festival
Chulha	Hearth
Chumban	Offering of gifts after marriage ceremony
Chaurai	A leafy vegetable akin to spinach
Churi	A witch

D

Dalya	Oats of vulgar wheat supplied and distirибuted by CARE
Dapla	One sided drum
Daru	Liquor
Daruna	Scare-crow
Daunri	Thrashing
Dehari/Dih	A sub-group of the Korwa living in plains
Derhwa	A form of loan in kind or cash
Dewar	Diviner
Dhania	Coriander (*Coriandrum sativum*)
Dhanu	Bow
Dhawra	Anogessus latifolia
Dhota	The pit dug for burial
Dhoti	Loin-cloth
Dhuku	A form of marriage in which a girl starts living with her lover's parents against the latter's will till the marriage is regularised
Doli	Hallowed trunk of a tree used as a protection to young saplings

Dona	Leafy cup used as a receptacle for eating food
Doomar	Figs
Dumkach	A marriage dance

G

Gaddi	Unauthorised liquor shops
Gaibar	Cow-shed
Gauntia	A village officer responsible for collecting land revenue during feudal rule in Surguja.
Ghar-jawain	A man living with wife's parents
Gondli	*Panicum miliare*
Gora-hudoo	Paddy sown by transplanting
Grihat	Petty landlords-cum-traders
Guria	Bead necklace

H

Handi	Home made beer brewed from rice and/ millets
Hansia	Sickle
Hardi Charhana	Massage of turmeric upwards
Hardi Utaarna	Massage of turmeric donwards
Harra	Terminalia chebula
Harwaha	Agricultural labour
Hookah	Hubble-bubble
Hudoo	Paddy

J

Jagra	Beer brewed from *mahua* (Bassia latifolia)
Janta	Roundish grinding stone
Jamun	A fruit (*Eugenia jambolana*)
Jantgi	An oil-seed (*Carthamus tinctorius*)
Janwai	Daughter's husband
Jati Panchayat	The traditional council of elders (*sayana*)
Jinhor	Maize
Johar	Paying of regards
Juath	Yoke

K

Kachnar	Buds of a tree used as vegetable

Kakkai	Wooden comb
Kamun	Purificatory bath taken after death
Kanya	Bride
Kapphan	Coffin
Kapuna	An under-garment worn by women
Kathal	Jack-fruit (*Artocarpus integrifolia*)
Katde boenta	Thrashing by feet
Kauh	Terminalia arjuna
Kelwa	Mid-day meals
Khaini	A concoction prepared by mixing lime with tobacco
Khanti	Dibble
Kharha	Rabbit (lepus cuniclus)
Kharyan	Granary
Khatang	A variety of maize
Kheencha phanda	A bird trap
Khirni	A fruit
Kiyari	A patch of land for cultivation of wet paddy
Koomba	A leafy hut
Kotri	Wild goat
Kurthi	Dolichos biflorus
Kusum	Schleichera trizuga

L

Lassa-phanda	A gum trap used for trapping birds
Lhasora	A fruit
Looga	Sari
Lota	Pitcher filled with beer for ceremonial drinking
Lotadar	A regional official of the Korwa *Jati Panchayat* who raises the pitcher for ceremonial drinking of beer in order to reunite the ostracized and those polluted owing to death of a family member.
Lotni	Black mustard (Brassica nigra)

M

Madia	Eleusine Coracona

Madua Platform erected for celebrations of a marriage
Mahua Bassia latifolia
Makhur Tobacco
Mandar Double sided drum
Mandra Fishing trap
Mangabara Engagement
Mantra Incantation
Marghat Burial ground
Massan A vampire
Mattha Butter-milk
Mewa Papaya (*Carica papaya*)
Mitti Korai Ceremonial digging of soil by priest before marriage
Moonr maati Clay used for cleaning and washing hair
Mua-ka-rasta The track through which a corpse is taken for burial

N

Namdhin Bow string
Naasta Breakfast served to members of a marriage party
NEFA North East Frontier Agency
Nilgai Bos-Elephas tragocamelus

P

Pahari Korwa The Hill Korwa
Palas *Butea Frondosa*
Panch The member of Jati/Statutory Panchayat
Panchayat Council of elders (*sayana*)
Panchpatri The punitive feast
Pandki Dove
Paani kaatna Marriage ceremony in which a pot filled with water is tossed and broken in air by a single blow of axe over the heads of a newly married couple
Parti Waste rocky land
Patni Oil crusher
Peepar A tree

Petla	Leveller
Phani	Leafy cup used for drinking liquor and beer
Pir-deo	Deities responsible for causing ailment if not propitiated properly
Pitar-deo	Ancestral family responsible for welfare of the family
Phar	Share of a plough

R

Rahar	*Cajanua indicus*
Rasia	A young vigorous male dancer
Renu-jari	A concoction of herbs used for fermenting beer
Rupni	A young astute female dancer

S

Sagai	Remarriage
Sahukar	Traders from Haryana and Rajasthan settled in tribal areas
Sajha	A form of share-cropping
Sakhua	Shorea-robusta
Sambhar	Cervus Unicolom
Sarpanch	Chairman of Statutory Panchayat
Sarson	Yellow mustard
Sawal-jawal	Dialogues preceding marriage
Sayana	An elder
Serali	A mlllet
Sukh-sarha	Bride-price
Super	Winnowing fan

T

Tabal	An axe
Tangi	Small axe
Tangna	Attachment
Tarki	Ear plugs
Tendu	Terminalia belierica

Til	*Sesamum indicus*
Tokni	A small basket

U

Urharia	A form of irregular marriage in which a married man elopes and remarries with a married woman or a virgin.

Index

Agriculture, 5, 6, 7
  Activities, 136
  Implements, 34, 35
  Lentils, 138
  Maize, 138-39
  Millets, 137-38
  Oil seeds, 136-37
  Paddy, 138
  Tribal practice of, 6
Ahmad, S.S.H., 18
Allami, Abul Fazl, 15
Animal husbandary, 134-35
  Cowdung, 135
  Goat grazing, 134-35
Animal trapping, 131
Animal wealth, 118-20
  Cows, 122
  Goats, 123
Apte, J.S., 5

Bailey, F.G., 3
Bansajhal, 9, 58
  Marriage method at, 58
Barnett, H.G., 3
Belshaw, 3
Bennet, John W. 3
Bhaduri, M.B., 18
Bhandari, J. S., 18
Borded labour, 183

Capital formation, 117-20
  Animal wealth, 118-20
  Livestock & poultry, 117, 120
  ornaments, 117

Census of India 1901, 18
Chattisgarh, 6
Chattopadhyaya, K.P., 5
Clans
  Bhaiyar, 74-75
  Functions of 72-74
  Origin of 71-72
Cook, Scott, 3
Credit facilities, 184
Crooks, J.W., 18, 19

Danda, A.K. 2, 3, 6, 181
Dalton, E.T., 2, 14, 18, 19, 21, 23
  Kamun, 69-70
De Brett, E.A., 18, 19
Dih/Danr Korwa, 70
Dress & Adornment, 35
Drinking water, 138, 182
Drinks & Narcotics, 38-39
  Handi, Traditional drink, 38-39
  Raw tobacco, 39
Driver, W.H.P., 18
Dube, A.L., 20
Dube, S.C., 5
Dutta, Majumdar, 5

Economic
  Market, 2, 3
  Methodological approach of, 2
  Non-market economy, 2-3, 180-85
Economic change, 167-68
  Earthen ware replaced, 175

Money mdium of exchange, 175
Economic exploitation, 159, 183, 185
Network of, 159-65
Economic relationship, 147-65
Educational facilities, 182
Primary schools, 184
Employee-Employer relationship (Grihat), 147-53, 162, 164, 165, 174
changing attitude of, 149
Equipment & Implements, 32-35
Arrow, 32
Axe, 32, 33
Box, 32
Digging sticks, 32
Fishing Traps, 33, 34
Epstein, Scarlett, 3
Family system, 75-76
Duties & privileges in, 86-87
Ego types, 80-83
Laterally extended, 78-79
Lineally extended, 76-78
Nascent, 76
Nuclear, 76
Polygynous, 79-80, 13
Residence after marriage, 85
Size of, 85
Firth, Raymond, 3
Fishing, 131-37
Food gathering, 125-26, 167
Food habits, 36-38
Beef, 38
Fruits, 37
Hearth, 36
Millets, 37
Tubers, 37
Forest, 103-05
Contractors, appointment in, 179
Deities, 103
Edible products from, 127-30
Digging tubers, 129-30
Gular fruit, 128
Kaltha fruit, 128
Mahua flowers, 127, 128
Mango, 128
Eviction from, 180
Nonedible products, 126-27
Fruits, 127
Fuels, 126, 172
Leaves, 127
Policy, 103, 104, 167
Gait, E.P., 18
Haimendorf, Von Furer, 5
Hill Korwas, 70
Methods of Study on, 8-11
Establishment Rapport, 9-11
Settlement of, 13
Suggestions & prospects of, 179-86
Hiralal, R.B., 18, 19
Horticulture, 135-36
Housing, 29-32
Architecture of, 31
Permanent, 29, 30
Raw material for, 31
Readymade, 180
Temporary, 29, 30
Hunting, 104, 130, 31, 167, 172
Prohibition of, 173
Husain, S., 5
Hutton, J. H., 18, 19
Hygiene & cleanliness, 35-36
Illiteracy, 159
Indebtedness, 153-55
Indian Forest Act 1927, 172
Initiation, 43
Jajmani type, 159
Kaplan, David, 3
Kinship system, 87-90
Denotative terminology, 87, 89-90
Korwa
Economic activities of, 125-46
Economic relationship, 147-65
Economic resources, 103-24
Language, 22-23
People, 29-102
Place of origin, 21-22
Rulers & Administrators, 18

1. An elderly Chief (*mukhya*).

2. A Nascent household.

3. A nuclear household.

9. Preserving a young sapling by planting it inside a hollowed tree-trunk (*doli*).

10. A young bride.

11. A marriage party in progress.